ADAM BLEVINS

Welcome To The S.H.I.F.T. Show:

How To Love Yourself In A World That Won't

To the unseen, unheard, and underestimated. The fighters in the dark. The ones knocked down, but who rose anyway.
For my wife—my partner, my mirror, my reason to be better.
For my son—our wolf, my greatest fight.
For Adaryn—our Raven, forever in my soul.
For BB—your last breath lives on through me.
For my mom, dad, and sisters—my foundation, my strength.
This book is for you.

Contents

Preface

This book is not here to coddle you. It's not another feel-good, Pinterest-quote, love-and-light manifesto wrapped in toxic positivity with hollow affirmations.

This book is real.

It's raw. It's a S.H.I.F.T. Show.

Because sometimes, life sucks. People are complicated. Trauma leaves scars. The world is a burning dumpster fire of contradictions, and most of us are just out here barely holding it together, pretending we've got it all figured out.

We don't. But you're not as stuck as you may think you are.

You've just been conditioned to believe you are. Fear not. This isn't the kind of conspiracy book where I try to convince you that some extraterrestrial forces are playing with your head. I am going to tell you about the real shit. The things that tear you down, yourself included.

This book is about taking your power back. Or realizing you have any at all. It's about seeing through the bullshit, dismantling the narratives that have kept you small, scared, playing by rules you never agreed to, and choosing to be your damn self finally. The S.H.I.F.T. Framework ™ isn't just a catchy acronym; it's a lifeline. It's the wake-up call you didn't ask for but desperately need.

It's the permission slip you've been waiting for to stop waiting, stop doubting, and start living like you belong in your own damn life. Because you do, but you might've been conditioned to forget it.

FYI, are you looking for a soft, gently whispered, "woosah" kind of self-help book? This may not be for you. Expect harsh language and a loud hype man screaming in your ear. This book will challenge you. It will likely cause you to question things you thought you knew. There will be moments that hurt and moments that heal. There will be moments when you're ready to cuss me out and others where you'll want a hug. Before you turn these pages, know that none are intended to harm you. They are intended to open your eyes, tickle your soul, and remind you of your worth and the worth of others. So, if you're ready to laugh, get uncomfortable, finally call out the bullshit, and learn to love yourself in a world that won't, then;

Welcome To The S.H.I.F.T. Show™.

Praise for Welcome to the S.H.I.F.T. Show™

★★★★★

"A game-changing book that challenges everything you thought you knew about self-worth... equal parts tough love and deep wisdom. An original approach to 'self-help for people who hate self-help.'"

— K.C. Finn, Readers' Favorite

★★★★★

"A must-read for anyone struggling to deal with the unpredictable nature of this world. Blevins offers hard-hitting truths with an unapologetic, engaging style that makes real-world wisdom accessible, and necessary."

— Pikasho Deka, Readers' Favorite

★★★★★

"Packed with practical insights and raw truths, this book empowers readers to rewrite their stories with strength and clarity. A bold and unfiltered guide to reclaiming identity in a broken world."

— Courtnee Turner Hoyle, Readers' Favorite

"A concrete, even coarse, approach to self-empowerment and personal fulfillment... Blevins' S.H.I.F.T. Framework™ is a no-nonsense blueprint backed by real-world trauma experience and research-driven insight. For those tired of hollow affirmations and looking to actually change,this is it."

— Kirkus Reviews

I

PART I: WELCOME TO THE SHIT SHOW

From birth, the world had a script written for you. Who to be, how to think, and where you fit. No questions asked. But what happens when that script makes you miserable? Part One rips apart the illusions, the conditioning, and the quiet lies shaping your reality. Society, identity, power, division, it's all on the table. Before changing anything, you must see the game for what it is. Once you do? There's no going back.

1

CHAPTER 1: WELCOME TO THE SHIT SHOW

Disclaimers: If spicy language, harsh truths, reasoning, love, kindness, compassion, vulnerability, and simple human decency offend you, put this book back on the shelf. You won't find much here. For everyone else, Welcome to the S.H.I.F.T. Show™. Several years ago, when I was going through one of the most challenging times of my life, I began putting my thoughts right here, right on these pages. As time passed and I healed, this project found its way onto the shelf of another abandoned ADHD project. Then, the world started changing, and people somehow got worse. Today? Today is the day people need to see the words on these pages. Additionally, there will be times throughout this book where you'll think, "Did he say that already"? "Haven't we already talked about this topic?" "Why does he keep saying that?" Pay attention to the words you see repeatedly. They are words you've likely ignored for far too long and thus, may feel foreign to you. Because here's a secret. All the things you don't like about yourself, others, your self-doubt, your anxieties, your fears, they all started as a thought. Those thoughts became ideas, those ideas became beliefs because you repeated them over and over until they felt like truth. That "truth" is what guides your behaviors, which guides your actions, which guides your entire existence.

So again, pay attention to what you repeatedly see. If there is anything in your life that you want to S.H.I.F.T., you'll need seeds planted that reinforce the ideas you need for your growth to be successful. I intend to be your gardener. I am going to whisper, repeatedly into your ears that you're worthy, valuable, capable, better, smarter, stronger, and more badass than what the lies behind your eyes have convinced you. I'm going to remind you of the space you deserve to take up. If you get to a page and feel like you've turned down this road already, let it happen. That's how narratives change. Repetition. Because those nasty thoughts in your head, they didn't happen overnight. Changing them won't either.

If you picked this up looking for a perfectly packaged, pastel-colored self-help manual that tells you to "just breathe" your way through life's BS, you might as well put this back on the shelf. This isn't a guided meditation, and I'm not here to hold your hand while you "align your energy" and manifest good vibes. I'm here only to rip off the blindfold you've been wearing and show you precisely what you're up against. Whether you realize it or not, you're already in the middle of the fight for your peace, joy, and right to be who the hell you want to be.

Here's a tiny hint about what this book is about: We, you, me, them, all of us spend too much time changing ourselves for other people and trying to change others for ourselves. But before you even get to that part, I need you to sit with something real quick.

Do you ever notice how people love to nod along when they hear something that fits what they already believe? They soak it up like gospel, repost it, shout it from the rooftops. But the second something challenges them, something that makes them feel, or question, suddenly, it's "too much." Suddenly, people are "too sensitive." Nah. Maybe you're just too comfortable!

Because the truth is, people don't just fear change. They fear being wrong. They fear that moment when something hits too close to home, and they have to ask themselves, Shit... have I been part of the problem? But you'll never grow if you only listen to the words that make you feel good and agree with. And if you never grow, you'll spend your whole life stuck in the same cycle, blaming the world for the person you refused to become.

So, before you turn the page, ask yourself: Are you here to see the world for what it is, or are you just here to feel validated? Because whether you like it or not, the world doesn't care what makes you comfortable. It feeds off complacency. The truth exists whether you acknowledge it or not. And the truth is? The world isn't just broken. It's filled with good people and cruel ones—proof that light and darkness aren't places; they're choices.

Which one are you?

Ready to sit with that question? Ready to ponder every choice, every action, every moment where you decide whether you'll be the light that mends or the shadow that consumes? Because, in the end, the world is neither good nor bad. It is only a reflection of what we choose to make it. You in?

Who the Hell Are You to Tell Me About Self-Help?

You may think, "Who are you, and what qualifies you to tell me anything about my life?"

Fair point.

The answer is nobody. I am nobody to tell you how to live your life, how to treat other people, or how to treat yourself. I have dedicated my professional life to public service and understanding the phenomenon of human beings. I am also guilty of most of the things you are about to read and aware enough to know that I'll mess up again. I have worked across more walks of life than most people see in a lifetime. I've been the guy making pizzas, the kid behind the gas station counter, pushing food carts in a nursing home. I've walked through jail cells, stood on crime scenes, and knocked on doors that would change lives forever. I've held people together when their worlds shattered and sat with those without anyone left to sit with them.

I have stood between chaos and control as a former detention officer and a state trooper. I have seen humanity at its breaking point, both in the people I arrested and those I tried to save. I have walked alongside first responders, helping them navigate the kind of trauma that stains your soul and never entirely washes out. I've held the hands of grieving families, stood in the wreckage of shattered lives, and delivered news that would split anyone's reality in two.

Then, I stepped into mental health. Because I didn't just want to respond to the damage; I wanted to help people heal. I am currently a resident in counseling, working with those who have carried the weight of trauma, grief, and self-doubt for far too long. I am pursuing a PhD in trauma-informed care, not because I wanted another title but because I wanted to understand. To break apart what destroys us, what rebuilds us, and why some people find their way back while others don't. I've spent my life walking the line between destruction and redemption, and I know firsthand what it feels like to be on both sides.

Yeah, I've got the credentials. I am a former state trooper, operations director of a nonprofit supporting first responders, resident in counseling, PhD student, but none of that is why I'm here. A degree doesn't teach you what it feels like to sit in your car at 2 AM, staring at the dashboard, wondering if it's even worth it anymore. A job title doesn't prepare you for the way trauma rots you from the inside out when you ignore it long enough. What brings me here? Experience. Perspective. The shit I've seen, the shit I've done, the people I've buried, and the nights I barely survived myself. I've seen the depths of human despair and the impossible resilience that rises from it. I've seen people at their absolute worst and broken, hopeless, standing on the edge of a choice they can never take back. And I've seen those same people claw their way back from the darkness, proving that even when everything feels lost, something remains left to fight for.

I've also seen the best parts of life. The ones that don't make headlines. The quiet, powerful moments that remind you why it's all worth it. The kind of love that makes you feel like you matter, not because of what you do, but simply because you are. I know this because I have it. I have a wife who sees the real me, even when I don't see myself. A woman who holds space for all the chaos, the scars, the restless mind that never entirely shuts off and loves me through it. She reminds me that strength isn't just pushing forward; it's knowing when to rest, feel, and just be.

My son doesn't care about my credentials or what I've survived. To him, I'm just Daddy. His hero, his protector, his playmate, the guy who will always be there to lift him onto my shoulders so he can see the world from a better view. He is my why. He reminds me that no matter how dark the world gets, there is always light.

I have a daughter I never got to hold. The weight of that loss is something I'll carry forever. It's an ache that sits just beneath the surface. Silent, but never absent. I think about her in the quiet moments, the space between laughter, and the questions that will never have answers. She changed me without ever taking a breath, made me a father in a way I never expected, and taught me that love isn't measured in time but in the space it leaves behind. I'll never know the sound of her voice or the way her hand would fit in mine, but she is still here. In the love I give, in the moments I refuse to take for granted, in the way I hold onto the people still within reach, I take her with me.

I have a family that has shaped me. Parents who raised me to stand for something, to question everything, to never back down from what I believe in. Siblings who remain my people, roots, history, first best friends, and introductions to the love of a blended family. I have friendships that run deeper than just shared laughs and good times. I've sat across from people who have been through their own Hells. People who have lost, suffered, and come out the other side, and through those connections, I've learned that healing doesn't come from pretending shit is okay. It comes from saying, "I see you; I hear you, I'm here.

For all the horror I've witnessed and vicariously carried, I've also seen beauty that can't be explained, only experienced. I've seen people forgive the unforgivable. I've seen strangers show up for one another in moments where they had no reason to. I've seen laughter in places where no one had any business laughing, but they did anyway because sometimes that's the only thing keeping you upright. I've learned that pain and joy aren't opposites. They coexist. They dance. You don't just get one or the other; you get both. The trick isn't avoiding the pain. It's knowing that the joy is still there, even when it's buried under the weight of everything else.

I have personally swept the floors in the pit of despair, and rock bottom is often paved with perspective. That part of my life is a difficult chapter, but it's worth the read. I have learned to use that chapter of my life to influence the stories of others. To show them the truth of life. The good, nasty, ugly, beautiful, complex, easy, meaningful, useless, and downright absurd truths of life. Do I know everything? Hell no. If you truly knew me, you'd laugh at that. However, the conversations that taught me the most were with people who felt they had no one to talk to. I hope their stories can open your eyes to a world unseen through me. A world of perspective. The world we all keep sweeping under the rug. A world in desperate need of reflection, and if this book helps one person, the juice is well worth the squeeze.

That's who I am.

This isn't another fluffy, feel-good self-help script. It isn't about quick fixes or empty positivity. This is about surviving a mentally dangerous world. This is about fighting back against everything designed to keep you trim, broken, and doubting yourself. I've been in the trenches. I've seen the worst of humanity and the best of it, and if there's one thing I know for sure, it's this: You are not weak. You are not broken. You are not beyond saving.

The world will try to convince you otherwise. It will tell you that you have to play by its rules, that you have to accept the labels it slaps on you, and that you have to stay in whatever box it shoves you into. But me? I'm going to tell you the damn truth. You don't have to stay small. You don't have to accept bullshit, and you sure as hell don't have to keep waiting for permission to take back control of your own damn life. Because life isn't just suffering. It's not just a struggle. It's not just survival. There is joy here, too. There is meaning. There is connection. There is purpose. There is love, even when it's complex to see, and, just maybe, if we all stopped long enough to look at each other, at this messy, complicated, brutal, beautiful world, we could start making it better.

Consider this. If we all stopped what we were doing, looked at the person nearest us, and asked, "How are you?" "Everything okay?". What would happen? What would the ripple effect be? How would the world change in five minutes if we all collectively gave a shit for five seconds? How many people would consider giving it "one more day"? How many people would survive just because you opened your mouth?

The World You Were Thrown Into

Look around. Look. What do you see?

I see a world where people care more about being correct than decent, where billionaires hoard wealth like dragons while kids starve to death. Where people use religion as an excuse to be cruel rather than as a reason to be kind, where hate spreads faster than wildfire, and empathy is treated like weakness. I see people cutting ties over political Facebook arguments while the people in power sit back and laugh, watching us tear each other apart. It's like we're all crabs in a bucket, and anytime one of us tries to climb out and break free, the others pull them right back down.

I see you.

I see people who've been kicked, beaten, and broken by life. Told they don't matter, told they'll never be enough, told to sit down and shut up, and I see them start to believe it. I see people shrinking, hiding, and playing small because they think they have no choice, like a bird born in a cage that eventually stops trying to fly. After all, it only knows life behind wires. I see people waking up every day hating themselves because so many factors, both external and internal, have convinced them of bullshit that isn't true. I see people who hate others for things they don't understand. I see people wasting their potential, their happiness, their whole damn existence because they're too scared to stand up and say, "Enough. It's time to be me."

I am SICK of watching a country, society, and world squander such incredible beauty and opportunity for power, greed, division, and, you guessed it, bullshit! I see so many people with blindfolds on and a blatant disregard for humanity. People celebrate the pain and demise of others while the rest of us sit back and say, "I'm not getting involved." Well, I'm incapable of keeping my mouth shut. So, America, society, the world, and you. We need to talk. We don't even know what we're capable of. Not even close. How do I know? Homo sapiens (humans), to the best of our knowledge, have been around for around 200,000 years (depends who you ask), and we still haven't collectively figured out how to be nice to each other. We think we can achieve world peace, have perfect economies, and a society that'll sustain itself while we keep punching each other in the face.

We all want to be free and happy, but we damn sure aren't doing a good job of building a world that allows us to do that. Instead, many are trying to create a world where some are "allowed" to be free and happy, while others spend centuries trying to convince others they breathe the same air. We judge each other relentlessly. We pretend to know what's best for everyone but ourselves repeatedly.

Some of you may have already judged me because of the language you've encountered thus far. Well, if you had any idea how much trauma lives behind those sentence enhancers, your self-righteousness may pass out. I get it if people don't like cuss words, but consider this. If tiny words not directed at you with malicious intent send you into a tailspin, is my language your concern? Or your reaction to it? I'm not trying to pick a fight; I'm here to help because I care about you. Let's not let my inability to express emotion without cussing get in your way of learning a few things. Friends? Let's roll. You may have even considered putting this book down when you saw that I was a former trooper. I get it. I won't try to convince you that I am one of the good ones. Your opinion of me would likely not occupy my thoughts for very long. However, I don't care at all where you come from. I want to see you flourish! I don't need your license and registration. I need your attention.

The Truth You Need to Hear

No one is going to hand you a better life. No one is going to swoop in and save you. You have two choices, keep letting the world and its endless stream of bullshit dictate your happiness, or grab the reins and take control. No more excuses. No more waiting for permission. No more pretending everything's fine when it's not—no more treating vulnerability like some virus while toxic, deluded behaviors are treated like an ice cream party. If you're ready to get real. Good. If you're tired of being lied to, manipulated, and trapped in a cycle of self-doubt and fear. You've made it to the right place. If you are perfectly comfortable refusing to see beyond the surface of yourself, others, and the world, you may find a YouTube binge more appropriate. Because I need people ready to see the world change for the better. And that? It starts with each of us. So, either get on board or get the hell out of the way.

This book isn't here to sugarcoat shit for you. It's here to wake you up. It shows you that no matter how disorderly, broken, or chaotic your life feels, you still have the power to take charge. It's here to change the rhetoric in your brain to serve you and others better. It is here to call you out, to lift you up, and to inspire confidence in you to be unapologetic in who you are despite the bullshit the world tries to sell you. Start investing in yourself because you fucking matter. Tell me in a few chapters if you still don't believe that.

You Were Never Broken. The World Is

But before we move forward, you need to understand something. You were not born broken. The world? Oh, this place was screwed up long before you got here. From the second you took your first breath, the world had already decided what you should be, how you should act, what you should believe, who you should love, what God you should pray to, and exactly where you fit into its neat little categories. It didn't ask you. It didn't give you a chance to figure it out for yourself.

It shoved you into a whirlwind of rules, labels, expectations, and a never-ending circus of bullshit, all disguised as "the way things are." Here's the issue. This means that most of who you are is predetermined based on the experiences, ideologies, and morals of those who came before you. Long before you had any opportunity to explore your thoughts, ideas, and understandings. I'll tell you this: I am not ashamed to admit that I am not the same person I was 5 years ago, 10 years ago, or 20 years ago. I learned and experienced things during those periods and noticed things that altered my perspective. Because I am open to it. I used to be that person. The one who took one look at another person and determined in my mind that I knew their story, what was best for them, and judged them before knowing anything at all about them. I refuse to be that person again and look through a restricted lens. That's where the bullshit starts.

Because what happens when "the way things are" makes you miserable? What happens when society tells you who to be, and you realize that person isn't you? What happens when you wake up one day and realize that every expectation is placed on you by your family, culture, politics, job, and the internet?

It isn't just exhausting; it's suffocating. It's like being handed a puzzle, but all the pieces are the wrong shape, and no matter how hard you try, they don't fit together. That's what this first part is about—the Shit Show.

The one that convinced you that you're not enough. The one that tricked you into believing you're supposed to have it all figured out. The one that keeps people fighting, divided, and miserable while pretending that's "life." The one that hurt you and has since convinced you to stay down. But let me tell you something that might piss off every system designed to keep you small: You don't have to play by their rules. Don't take that as an encouragement to go and rob a bank. I'm not telling you to be a criminal. I'm encouraging you to rebel against every factor in life that tries to fit you into a mold that wasn't made for you!

The Shift Starts Now

This book isn't about "fixing" you. Because you are not a broken toy that needs to be fixed. You are a human being, living a human experience with human problems and human bullshit. We like to pretend there's another realm or reality between us, the truth, and those we try to impress. One where we are always either below or above what's acceptable. This is about undoing the conditioning, the lies, and the bullshit that has kept you locked in a cycle of self-doubt, guilt, and pressure to be someone you're not. This is about bringing those questions up from your subconscious, the ones you've always been resistant to address, and giving them room to explore. This is about being you.

To kick this thing off, we're gonna pull back the curtain

on all the things that have been screwing with your head. We're gonna talk about the systems and structures that shape your reality. Society, politics, family, friendships, identity, social media, beliefs, and the constant war between facts and opinions. We'll lay it all out, no sugarcoating or tiptoeing around feelings. We will shine light into the darkest, most conditioned corners of our minds and face the complex topics we all like to pretend don't exist. We will have uncomfortable conversations from which we are constantly shying away. We are going to call out hate and division with love and unity. We are going to call out judgment with compassion and bias with understanding. This is where we call it what it is.

Because the truth is, you can't shift your life until you understand what's been holding you back. Make no mistake, some of the things you've been told to believe, to follow, to obey? They were never meant to serve you. They were designed to control you. But not anymore. You will see the world differently when we're done with part one. Once you know the game and what it is, you can't unsee it.

This book is not designed with the intent to harm or offend you. It's designed to challenge you with the intent of showing you that you're better, stronger, and more valuable than you think.

Put your boots on.

You've just entered the Shit Show.

2

CHAPTER 2: SOCIETY—A BEAUTIFULLY GIFT-WRAPPED SHIT SHOW

Let's be honest, society can sometimes be a massive pile of warm shit. Not in a 'people make mistakes' kind of way, but in a 'five-car pileup during rush hour in a snowstorm kind of way. If you've ever felt like something about this world doesn't make sense, like you're running a race with no finish line, like you're constantly being judged, like no matter what you do, it's never enough, you're not imagining it. Society is built to make you feel that way.

From the moment you were born, you weren't just learning how to walk and talk; you were being indoctrinated. The "rules" were already in place, the expectations were locked in, and your job was to fall in line without question. And God forbid you challenge anything because then society slaps you with a label: Difficult. Disruptive. Rebellious. Wrong. Or my personal favorite," a problem."

Well, guess what? **You Should Be a Problem.**

Society wasn't built to make you happy, and the world continues to build itself against you. It was built to keep you in line, conformable, and static. Imagine society as one of those rigged carnival games. You know, the ones that look fair but are designed so you never win? You throw the ball; it bounces off some invisible barrier. You take your best shot, and the hoop is just too small. And the guy running the game? He's standing there, grinning ear-to-ear, telling you to try again, knowing damn well the game is stacked against you. Notice the shock on their face when you win. Life is the same. When you rise above the nonsense and try to change the tides, they look at you like you're a unicorn. Well, sharpen your horn, sweetheart; it ain't none of their damn business. From the minute you take your first breath, the game is already set up, and if you don't start leading instead of just playing along, you'll be stuck throwing balls at a rigged hoop forever. Spending your hard-earned singles on an impossible game when you could eat funnel cake instead.

How Societal Expectations Are Built to Make You Feel Like You're Never Enough

Here's the game you were thrown into without reading the rulebook:

You're Supposed To Look A Certain Way

But you're vain if you care "too much" about your appearance. If you don't care enough, you're a mess. Either way, you lose. Spend too much on skincare, gym membership, or clothes, and people will say you're shallow. Let yourself exist naturally;

suddenly, you've "let yourself go." Oh, and don't forget, your value will still be measured by the standards you're criticized for trying to meet.

You're Supposed To Be Successful.

But not too successful, or people will resent you. Also, don't struggle too much, or people will think you're lazy. Hustle, but not too hard. Make money, but not so much that people start whispering about how you "must've had help." Be ambitious, but not in a way that makes others uncomfortable. Stay in your lane, but also "reach for the stars." And for the love of all things holy, don't you dare admit that sometimes you're exhausted.

You Should Follow Your Dreams

But only if they fit into a socially approved box. Want to be an artist? It's a cute hobby, but get a "real job." Want to be a lawyer? Well, now you're "selling your soul." Want to start a business? You better have a backup plan. Want stability? Now you're "playing it too safe." The only acceptable dream is the one everyone else agrees with, and even then, you'll still hear about how you're doing it wrong.

You Should Be Kind

But if you're too kind, people walk all over you. If you're not kind enough, you're a selfish asshole. Give too much, and people will expect it. Hold boundaries, and suddenly, you're cold and unapproachable. And let's not forget that kindness is only celebrated when it looks nice. Silent sacrifices don't count unless they can be turned into an inspirational social media post.

You Should Be Independent

But not too independent, or you'll be seen as "difficult." Have standards, but not too many. Be self-sufficient, but don't act like you don't need anyone. Stand on two feet, but don't be so good at it that you intimidate people. Be independent in a way that makes other people feel comfortable. Good luck figuring that one out.

You're Not Like The Rest

But you're a sellout if you're too much like the rest. Be unique, but only in a marketable way. Be different, but not too different, or people won't take you seriously. Have your own opinions, but not ones that make anyone uncomfortable. Stand out and fit in just enough that you don't make waves. It's a tightrope walk on a line that keeps moving, and no matter what, you'll never be enough for everyone.

It's an endless cycle of what the fuck. No matter what you do, there's always some expectation to make you feel like you're falling short. And that's the whole point. Keeping you in a constant state of insecurity is profitable. You'll try to buy your way into worthiness if you think you're insufficient. More clothes, courses, self-help books, memberships, and validation from external sources tell you this is what you need to be complete. They don't want you to be happy. They want you to keep searching for happiness everywhere they can sell it to you.

What if you stopped playing the game? What if you decided right now that you're already enough? What if you quit trying to win a rigged system and just started living?

Think About It—Who Wins If You Feel Good About Yourself?

How many industries would take a serious hit if people woke up and felt good about themselves? The diet industry wouldn't be raking in billions, convincing you that your body is a problem to be solved. The beauty industry wouldn't be able to sell you "flaws" they made up to profit off fixing them. The self-help industry wouldn't survive if people stopped believing they were broken and needed the next "life-changing" seminar. (Don't confuse this with practical interventions.) The plastic surgery industry wouldn't thrive off making you think aging is something to be ashamed of. The fashion industry wouldn't be able to guilt you into replacing your whole wardrobe every season to stay "on trend." The pharmaceutical industry wouldn't be making a fortune from medicating problems that sometimes come from a system designed to stress you out. A lot of industries depend on your insecurity. The worse you feel about yourself, the richer they get.

If society wanted you to feel happy and whole, it would have made it easier for you to do that. But it doesn't. It keeps moving the goalposts, ensuring that no matter how hard you try, there's always something missing. And if you don't feel like you're missing something, don't worry; society will be happy to remind you. Are you tired of people seeing the weird cartilage flaps on the side of your head? Yes, ears. Well, worry no more! Let me introduce you to Invisaears!! The stylish way to hide those hideous, shameful sound holes society has suddenly decided are a problem! For just $299.99, you can finally stop embarrassing yourself with your natural anatomy. But wait! Act now, and we'll throw in a bonus set of ear-reshaping tape because those freakish lobes could use some work, too! Sounds ridiculous? Good. Because that's precisely how marketing works.

One day, something about you is fantastic. The next day, some corporation decides it's unacceptable, and suddenly, there's a product designed to "fix" it. Your pores are too big. Your teeth aren't white enough. Your hair is the wrong texture. Your body isn't shaped right. Congratulations! You now have a brand-new insecurity you didn't even know existed! And when you think you've finally caught up, they move the goalpost again. What was trendy yesterday is "cringe" today. What was "natural beauty" is now unpolished. It's an endless cycle designed to keep you chasing an impossible standard so they can keep cashing in. It's like being on a treadmill that speeds up every time you catch your breath. What if you woke up, looked in the mirror, and liked what you saw? The whole system would crumble.

The Unspoken Rules Society Throws at You (and Why Most of Them Are Bullshit)

The wildest part? A lot of these expectations aren't even explicitly stated. They're just understood. Unspoken rules. They exist in the background, shaping how we think, act, and judge ourselves without anyone ever having to say them aloud. They're absorbed, passed down, and reinforced in ways we don't notice until we drown in them.

Like the unspoken rule that says:

You should have your life together by 25.

But also, you should be young and carefree. But also, you should be responsible. But also, wait, what do you mean you have anxiety? Why aren't you traveling the world? Why aren't you a homeowner yet? Why aren't you taking risks? Why aren't you playing it safe?

You should work yourself to the bone.

But don't forget self-care! But also, don't be lazy. But also hustle harder. But also, what do you mean you're burned out? Why don't you take a break? Why aren't you more productive? Why aren't you sleeping more? Why are you sleeping so much?

You should be in a relationship.

But don't rush! But also, don't be single for too long! But also, don't settle. But also, why are you still alone? Are you putting yourself out there? Are you focusing too much on dating? Are you focusing too much on yourself? Are you too picky? Are you not picky enough?

You should want kids.

But also, don't have them too early. But also, don't wait too long. But also, make sure you're financially stable first. But also, don't let money stop you from building a family. But also, don't have too many kids. But also, don't have too few. But also, wait, you don't want kids? How dare you!

You should be strong.

But also, be vulnerable. But also, don't be too emotional. But also express your feelings. But also keep them in check. But also, why don't you talk more? But also, why are you constantly venting?

You should know what you're doing with your life.

But also, don't be too rigid. But also have a plan. But also be spontaneous. But also, why are you still figuring things out? But also, why are you so set in your ways?

Society is obsessed with putting people into neat little categories and setting conflicting expectations within those categories so that no matter what you do, someone has something to say. It's like a never-ending game of "Gotcha!". And here's the kicker: none of these expectations will help you. They exist solely to keep you in constant doubt, questioning yourself at every turn. They're designed to make sure you never reasonably feel secure. Not in your appearance, not in your choices, not in your life. Because when people feel safe, they stop being controllable.

When you stop second-guessing yourself, you stop needing validation from everyone else. You start living life on your terms when you stop chasing arbitrary milestones. And when you stop believing you're somehow behind, you realize you were never on the wrong timeline, just someone else's. But people lose their minds the second you step outside these unspoken rules. Because if you decide not to play the game, suddenly, they're forced to confront the fact that the game is bullshit. And nobody likes realizing they've wasted their entire life following rules that never mattered.

What happens when you stop caring about their thoughts and start listening to yourself?

Freedom.

The Myth of "Normal"

"Normal" is the ultimate measuring stick. It's the standard you're supposed to live up to, even though no one can define what it means. It's the invisible line in the sand that you're expected to walk perfectly. Not too much this, not too much that, just the right amount of whatever makes you acceptable.

But acceptable to whom?

What's a "normal" body?

Is it the one in magazines? The one in fitness ads? The one that gets called "too skinny" in one breath and "too big" in the next? Is it the one that ages naturally or the one that's criticized for "letting go"? The one that follows trends dictated by billion-dollar industries profiting off insecurity?

What's a "normal" way to live?

Graduate, get a job, get married, buy a house, have kids? Rent forever because the economy is a joke? Stay single and travel the world? Work a 9-to-5? Quit the rat race and live off-grid? Every choice comes with someone waiting to tell you you're doing it wrong.

What's a "normal" career path?

Climbing the corporate ladder? Owning a small business? Freelancing? Being an artist? A doctor? A blue-collar worker? "Work smarter, not harder," they say until you do, and then they call you lazy. "Work hard," they say until you do, and then they call you a corporate drone. Ask five different people, and you'll get five different answers because "normal" doesn't exist. It's a made-up concept, constantly shifting depending on culture, time, and whoever holds the most power in a given moment. In the 1950s, "normal" was being a housewife. In the 1980s, "normal" was working yourself to death for a pension. In 2024, "normal" is pretending you're okay while you silently question everything. And tomorrow? "Normal" will benefit the people at the top the most. Normal is a moving target; if you spend your life chasing it, you'll never catch it because it isn't real. It's not tangible. It's an idea.

That's why the happiest people aren't trying to be "normal." They're the ones who said, "Screw it, I'm going to the grocery store in my pajamas." They're the ones who realize that no one is coming to hand them a permission slip to live the way they want to live. They're the ones who understand that breaking the mold doesn't make you a failure; it makes you free.

Think about it. Everyone who ever did something significant—the ones who changed the game, redefined success, or lived in a way that people envied—were initially told, "That's not normal." The people who fought for fundamental human rights? Not normal. The ones who built businesses from nothing? Not normal. The ones who rejected the idea that you need a traditional job, a traditional relationship, or a traditional anything to be happy? Not normal. And yet, here we are, benefiting from everyone who dared to be different.

So, what if instead of trying to fit into a definition that doesn't exist, you asked yourself: What do I want? Not what's expected of me. It's not what keeps other people comfortable. It's not what makes me look "successful" to people who don't matter. Because the second you start living by that answer, something incredible happens. You stop seeking permission. You stop apologizing for existing as you are. Stop wasting your life chasing a version of yourself that was never yours.

That's when you start living.

What Doesn't Give People the Right to Mistreat, Judge, or Marginalize Others

Nothing, and I mean nothing, gives us a free pass to treat other people like garbage. Not your faith. Not your politics. Not your upbringing. Not your culture. Not your trauma. Not your stress, your bad day, your rough childhood, or your zodiac sign. Your struggles? They are real. They are valid. But they don't give you a license to make life harder for someone else.

27

Your beliefs? They're yours. Believe them. But don't use them as a weapon to control or belittle others. Your pain? It's valid, but it doesn't justify causing more pain.

Look, we've all been through shit. Some more than others. Some of us have walked through hell and back and barely survived. But society loves giving people excuses to be assholes. "Well, that's just how I was raised." Cool. And? Suppose your upbringing includes treating people like second-class citizens because of their gender, race, religion, sexuality, mental health, or anything else they can't control. In that case, it's time to unlearn that shit. Uncomfortable yet? Good! You're ready.

You are responsible for what you do with the lessons you were taught. You don't get to decide someone else's worth based on your worldview. You don't get to dictate someone else's rights because you don't understand their reality. You don't get to dehumanize someone and then call it "just your opinion." And before you say, "But I have a right to my opinion," sure, you do. But opinions don't excuse harm. Opinions don't win wars. They start them.

Think about this. Right now, people are living in your country who do not have the same rights as you because of opinions. And let's be honest, some opinions aren't opinions. They're just well-packaged hate. If your "opinion" strips someone of their humanity, it's not an opinion. It's just being a dick. If your "opinion" actively takes away another person's rights, it's not an opinion. It's oppression. If your "opinion" is rooted in fear, ignorance, or misinformation, it's not an opinion. It's just the echo of everything you were told without questioning it. And when people call it out, there's always some excuse.

My personal favorite? "I have friends that are Black!" Oh, I love that for you, but it doesn't excuse the incredibly racist poison that just fell out of your face. Having a Black friend doesn't mean you're immune to racism any more than having a gay cousin makes you an LGBTQ+ ally. Relationships don't absolve you of prejudice. Your actions do.

So, let's put all preconceived notions and politics aside for a second and consider something with me. Imagine waking up today with rights, the same rights as your neighbor, your coworker, your friend. Now imagine waking up tomorrow and having those rights stripped away. Not because you committed a crime. Not because you did anything wrong. Not because you're dangerous or unworthy. Just because someone, somewhere, decided you shouldn't have them anymore. Because they don't like who you are. Because you don't fit into their worldview. Because someone with more power than you signed a document that told the world you are "less than." That would be shocking, right? You'd be angry, right? You'd fight back, right? Two weeks into 2025, Americans woke up to this reality. And this isn't hypothetical. This isn't just some slippery slope argument. This is happening right now. I don't care what your opinion is on transgender people. Let me say that again: I do not give a single shiny shit what your opinion is of them. Agree with them. Disagree with them. Who gives a shit? This isn't about agreement. It's about fundamental human rights. You don't have to understand someone's experience to respect their humanity. You don't have to agree with how someone lives their life to acknowledge that they deserve to live it. You don't have to relate to someone to recognize that they deserve the same freedom you take for granted. I have sat across from these people. Learning everything that makes them uniquely them. Learning how broken and confused they are. Not for the reasons you may be thinking, but because every single time they open their eyes, someone judges them, dismisses them, and hates them.

Here's an uncomfortable truth. Most people who hate, judge, and are intolerant of transgender people have never even spoken to one. They wipe their ass the same as you. They bleed like you. They feel like you. They hurt like you.
It's time to wake up and realize that we're all closer to each other than we think.

So, ask yourself this. Is how you feel about them more valuable than their rights? Food for thought. Chew on it. And if that question makes you uncomfortable? Good. It should. Because that means it's worth thinking about.

What Doesn't Give You the Right to Mistreat or Judge Yourself

Now, let's flip the script. Just like you don't have the right to tear others down, you also don't have the right to tear yourself down. Because you are not your worst moments. You are not your past. You are not the lies your inner critic whispers when no one else is around.

Here's what doesn't make you unworthy, broken, or beyond saving:
Your past mistakes.
You're not defined by your worst moments. Growth exists. You are allowed to learn. You are allowed to change. You can wake up tomorrow and choose to be someone better than you were yesterday.
Your mental health struggles.

Anxiety, depression, PTSD, trauma? They don't make you "less than." They make you human in an unforgiving world. You are not weak because your brain fights battles no one can see. You are not "too much" because you carry a weight others don't understand.

Your failures.

Failing doesn't mean you're a failure. It means you tried. It means you cared about something enough to go for it. The people who accomplish the most in life? They've failed more times than you can count. The only absolute failure is never trying at all.

Your body, your appearance, your weight

There is no "perfect" body. There is no other you. Be proud. Be grateful. This body has carried you through every single thing you've survived. That's not something to hate. That's something to honor.

How much money you make

Society might worship wealth, but your paycheck doesn't define your value. The wealthiest people in the world still die. The most successful people still struggle. If money determined worth, there wouldn't be billionaires in therapy.

Your relationships (or lack of them)

Single? Married? Divorced? Ghosted? Your relationship status isn't a personality trait. You are not a failure if you're single. You are not a better person just because you're in a relationship.

31

Your worth is not tied to whether someone else chooses you. Choose yourself.

What other people think of you

They don't have to like you. You don't have to enjoy them—the end. The world keeps turning. Someone will always have an opinion about you. Let them. It costs you nothing to ignore them and live your life on your terms.

The world will try to convince you that you're not enough. That you have to earn self-respect, self-love, and happiness. But guess what? You already deserve those things. Not because you "worked hard" for them. Not because you checked the right boxes. Not because you look a certain way, act a certain way, or play by society's nonsense rules. You deserve them because you exist. Because you are a human being, and that is enough.

So, stop waiting for permission to be kind to yourself. Stop searching for some imaginary moment when you finally "deserve" love, peace, or happiness because you don't need permission. You never did. You are the one who decides how this story goes from here. Society may think they've dealt you the cards, but you choose whether you sit at the table.

And if the table is built to make you feel small?

Flip the fucking table.

Let's Question Things

Have you ever seen that person who laughs at a girl with blue hair? Maybe you've been that person. I'm not scared to admit that I have. But here's the real question: why does it matter

32

to you? Instead of thinking, "Why does she have blue hair?" ask yourself, "Why do I give a shit?" See someone who's gay? Why do you care? Don't like someone because of their skin color? Why? Where did that come from? What did they do to you? Someone with tattoos? Is anyone drawing on you? No? Then why does their ink affect your life? Someone with mental health issues? Oh, I see. Is your life perfect? You've never struggled? Never questioned? Ever had a bad day? Don't like someone else's politics? Cool. Are they casting your vote? No? Then, move along. You have to ask yourself why something that has NOTHING TO DO WITH YOUR LIFE becomes so obsessive to you. Because here's the deal, when the most prominent thoughts in our mind is our disgust with anything that's different from us or our point of view, we've got bigger problems. Here's the bad news. It ain't her blue hair. It's our insecurity.

Let's get real for a second. How many times have you seen a 2-year-old white kid call the cops on a 2-year-old black kid because they were playing in the same sandbox? Probably never. Because they haven't learned to hate yet. All they see is another kid to play with. Imagine if we never lost that. But we do. Somewhere along the way, we start categorizing people. We begin assigning labels. We start deciding who is worthy and who is less than. And the worst part? Most of us don't even realize we're doing it. We get stuck in this head space where we see something unusual to us and assume that because it's distinctive, it's wrong. That they're wrong. But why?

Think about it. Your eyes are the only ones you see the world through 24/7. Your beliefs are the only ones in your head 24/7. If the only food you've ever eaten is chicken for five years, and then someone suddenly hands you duck nuts, you'll probably think, "What the hell is this?" Extreme analogy? Maybe. Same brain function? You bet. We reject what we don't know. We fear what we don't understand. And when we don't take the time to question why we think the way we think, we end up unthinkingly repeating the same toxic cycles.

So, let's ponder a question together.

Imagine for a moment that humanity resets. No history. No societal norms. No politics. No religion. No predetermined beliefs. Just people. Would racism still exist? Would communities still be marginalized? Would you give a rat's ass if someone told you they didn't believe they were male or female? No. Because you wouldn't know any of this shit yet. I'm sure after a little time we'd go right back to our same old hateful ways. But would you immediately look at a woman who's slightly larger than the rest and think, "Eww, that's not attractive"? Would you automatically assume that a tattooed person is unprofessional? Would you feel threatened by someone who worships differently than you? No. Because society wouldn't have planted those belittling bugs in your ear yet. Looking beyond the surface? That's a lost art.

So, here's where we're at: Society has conditioned you to believe you're never enough. It's built on contradictions, moving goalposts, and unspoken rules that exist solely to keep you in line. It gives you an illusion of "normal" that no one can define or live up to. And it profits from your insecurity. And now, you've got two choices:

You can keep following the script society handed you, trying to be "enough," chasing the ever-changing definition of success, and seeking approval from a system that never wanted you to win. Or you can throw the script in the trash and start writing your own rules. Because guess what? Whether you conform or you don't. Whether you change yourself to appease them or if you unapologetically live your own authentic life...

They will still find something wrong with you. You're too gay. You're too Christian. You're too liberal. You're too conservative. You're too loud, quiet, ambitious, passive, or something. And for what? Do they pay your bills? Do they wipe your ass? Do they call to see how you're doing? No?

Then ignore 'em. I don't know about you, but I'm not about to let a broken system tell me how to live.

But then again, I am a white, heterosexual male who, for most of my life, identified as a conservative Christian. So, no one ever tells me how to live. In the eyes of American standards, I'm the gold star. Slap a superiority sticker on my forehead and call me Uncle Sam. Societally, I have never been forced to question the ground I stand on. And that? That's a privilege. A statement everyone should be able to make. But they can't because the system wasn't built for everyone.

3

CHAPTER 3: POLITICS—THE BLOOD SPORT OF EGO, OUTRAGE, AND BULLSHIT

If you want to see human beings at their absolute worst, bring up politics at a family gathering. If that doesn't do the trick, go to the comments sections. That's usually where true colors come out to play. Watch in horror as your aunt, who barely knows how to operate Facebook, suddenly becomes a political analyst. See your uncle, who hasn't read a book in 40 years, confidently declare that he understands foreign policy's complexities better than experts. Observe as your cousin, who once got banned from Twitter for threatening a fast-food chain over a discontinued menu item, accuses the rest of the family of being "sheep." It's a Shit Show.

Politics used to be about policy, leadership, and (at least in theory) the greater good. Now, it's a team sport, except nobody wins, and the entire game is designed to keep people hating each other while the people in power sit back and laugh. Look at America today. It doesn't matter which side you ask; their answers will be the same. Both sides think the other is mentally handicapped, fascist, racist, and completely detached from reality. And common sense? Whichever way you vote, the other side has none.

Political Loyalty is the New Blind Faith

It's not just about policies anymore; it's about identity. People don't just support a party; they become that party. They wear it like a second skin, tattoo it onto their self-worth, and defend it with naive loyalty, usually reserved for cults. You can be as uncomfortable with that statement as you want, but ask yourself how you feel about the other party. Do you think they are blind, mindless puppets? I hate to burst your partisan bubble, but they believe the same about you. And just like with cults, questioning anything, even a little, is seen as betrayal.

Imagine two people arguing about which airline is better. One swears by Airline A, the other by Airline B. Both have had good and bad experiences. But instead of admitting that both airlines have strengths and weaknesses, they start screaming at each other like their lives depend on it. Now, imagine one of the airlines is run by corrupt executives who don't care about their passengers. Still, they know that as long as they keep people fighting over which airline is better, nobody will notice that the planes are falling apart.

How about this? Two people screaming at each other over which football team is superior. One is die-hard for Team Red, and the other swears by Team Blue. They argue about stats, championships, and which quarterback is the GOAT, refusing to acknowledge any flaws in their team or any strengths in the other. Now, imagine the owners of both teams secretly having dinner together, laughing over expensive steaks, knowing that no matter who wins, they always profit. They don't care about the fans; they stay distracted, loyal, and willing to fight for a team that wouldn't even notice if they disappeared.

That's modern politics. While we argue over jerseys, the people in charge are cashing in because as long as we stay divided, nobody's questioning the game itself. The second you make something your entire identity, you lose the ability to think critically about it. You stop questioning. You stop looking at nuance. You stop seeing people as people and start seeing them as enemies. You stop giving objective perspective a chance. This leads to hating someone you know nothing about aside from which jersey they're wearing.

Which is precisely what those in power want. And they're damn good at it.

How People Weaponize Political Beliefs to Excuse Being Assholes

One of the nastiest side effects of political division is how people use it as a free pass to be terrible human beings. Do you disagree with me? That means you're evil. You voted differently than me? You're the reason the world is falling apart. Did you dare to ask a question? You're part of the problem. It's lazy thinking wrapped in self-righteousness.

I have witnessed mutual friends of mine, people who have been friends for decades, who have carried each other's darkest secrets, who have stood by each other in tragedy, never speak again over a Facebook post. A. Fucking. Facebook. Post.

Read that again. Not over some deep personal betrayal. Not over a moment of actual harm. Not over something life-altering. A Facebook post. And somehow, this is normal now. People don't talk anymore. They declare who is worthy of existing in their world and who isn't. We've built this culture where disagreement isn't just a difference of perspective; it's grounds for war. Where critical thinking is dying because no one cares about nuance anymore, it's all just "Us vs. Them." Where the goal isn't even understood. It's just about winning.

Winning what, exactly? The most followers? The most likes? The most validation from strangers? A fake moral high ground that only exists inside the echo chamber you built for yourself? The world isn't better because people are cutting off lifelong friendships over one election, one news headline, and one manipulated soundbite. All it does is divide us further. And guess what? That's precisely the point. Because when people are separated, they're easier to control. A country of people who hate each other will never stand up together to fix real problems. If we're too busy fighting each other, we'll never fight the systems that thrive on our division.

Disagreement isn't war. Different perspectives aren't a threat. Someone questioning something you believe isn't an attack. And yet, people act like curiosity is treason. Like asking, "Are we sure this is the full story?" is the same as saying, "I'm siding with the enemy." We act like daring to consider another perspective makes us look weak. Newsflash: They weren't strong if your beliefs can't survive questions.

The people in power love watching us rip each other apart. Because every time we're screaming at each other, we're not paying attention to the people pulling the strings. Every time we're boycotting our neighbor's business over a stupid tweet, we're not boycotting the corporations that exploit us all. Every time we cancel someone over a disagreement, we're not holding actual criminals accountable. So, here's a radical idea: what if we stopped playing into it? What if we stopped letting politics turn us into people we don't even like? What if we stopped measuring someone's worth by the box they checked on a ballot? What if we stopped throwing away real friendships, authentic relationships, and honest conversations over whatever outrage was trending this week?

Because here's what no one wants to admit. Most of us have the same core values. Most want to live in a fair, safe, and just world. Most of us want to protect our families, have opportunities, and be treated with respect. We disagree on how to get there. And if you think screaming at people is the best way to change their minds, let me ask: has that ever worked on you? When were you last humiliated, insulted, or publicly shamed into changing your perspective? Exactly. It doesn't work. If anything, it just makes people dig their heels in deeper. Because once you publicly crucify someone, their pride won't let them admit they were wrong, even if they start to question it deep down.

That's why we're stuck. Because instead of having hard conversations, we cancel them. Because instead of listening, we scream. Because instead of trying to understand, we want to be correct. What if we choose differently? What if we gave people the space to grow? What if we challenged ideas without destroying people? What if we prioritized understanding over proving a point? Because the real enemy isn't the guy down the street, who voted differently than you. It's the billionaires who profit from our division. It's the politicians who manipulate us into fighting battles that benefit them. The systems keep us exhausted, overworked, underpaid, and too distracted to fight back. You don't have to agree with everyone. You don't have to accept ignorance, bigotry, or cruelty. But you have to ask yourself if how you engage with the world is making it better. If your beliefs only make you hate people you've never met, maybe it's time to re-evaluate who's benefitting from them.

Because it sure as hell isn't you.

Your Political Beliefs Do Not Automatically Make You a Good Person.

You can plaster all the correct slogans on your car, put the perfect hashtags in your bio, and vote exactly how your "side" tells you to, and still be an absolute garbage human. Why? Because morality isn't a team sport. It's personal. It's not about what group you belong to. It's not about which party you vote for. It's not about what labels you wear proudly in your social circles. It's about who you are when no one is watching. Some people claim to fight for equality while treating service workers like absolute shit. People who say they care about family values but haven't spoken to their mother in years. People who shout about freedom while actively trying to take it away from others. And yet, they all think they're the good guys.

Why? Because when people tie their morality to their political identity, they stop doing actual self-reflection. They don't have to. If their side is good, and they're on that side, then they must be good too, right? If you're convinced you're right, why consider anything else? Wrong. Being on the "right side" of history doesn't automatically make you a good person. Morality isn't about what party you vote for; it's about how you treat the people around you, especially the ones who can't do anything for you. You can spend your whole life holding all the "right" beliefs and still be a cruel, selfish, hypocritical asshole.

If you say you support mental health but shame people when they're struggling, you're a hypocrite. If you claim to love inclusivity but instantly shut down anyone who disagrees with you, you're a hypocrite. If you scream about "supporting the working class" but belittle a fast-food worker for getting your order wrong, you're a hypocrite. I am the world's guiltiest of that. If you post about kindness online but act like a complete asshole in real life, you're a hypocrite. Your "side" doesn't make you a good person. Your actions do.

The way you show up in the world, not just when people are watching, but in the quiet, unrecorded, unfiltered moments of your life. Do you listen when someone shares a perspective that challenges yours? Do you treat strangers with the same respect as your friends? Do you hold yourself accountable for your mistakes or pretend they didn't happen? Because here's a hard truth. Your ideology isn't a personality.

Wearing the right colors, saying the right buzzwords, and being on the "good team" does not automatically make you a good human. It's easy to call yourself compassionate. It's harder to practice patience with someone you don't under-stand. It's easy to share a hashtag. It's harder to put in the work to change something. It's easy to demand respect. It's harder to give it. Especially to those who don't see the world like you do.

So, here's a challenge: Stop assuming you're right just because your side told you so. Stop believing that because you vote a certain way, you're immune to being an asshole. Stop hiding behind labels and ask yourself if your actions align with the values you stand for. It's not about the slogans you shout; it's about the person you are. And if you think your political affiliation alone makes you a good person, I have bad news: You've already stopped thinking for yourself.

Being an Asshole in the Name of Your Beliefs Does Not Make You a Hero.

It makes you an asshole.

Let me explain.

It doesn't matter which wealthy manipulator you voted for. It doesn't matter what ideology you align with. It doesn't matter how many bumper stickers you have, how many hashtags you post, or how many arguments you've won online. If you use your political beliefs to target, hurt, bully, and belittle others, you're not a warrior for justice; you're just an asshole with a cause.

Standing for something doesn't require stomping on other people. You can believe your values without shoving them down people's throats like an overcooked steak. You can fight for justice without becoming the thing you claim to hate. You can advocate for your beliefs without acting like you're the second coming of morality. And yet, people act like being a self-righteous, condescending, insufferable jerk somehow makes them brave. No, Karen, you're not a hero because you screamed at a teenager over their political shirt at the grocery store. No, Brad, you're not a champion of democracy because you called your neighbor a traitor for voting differently than you. No, Kyle, you're not a warrior for freedom because you harassed someone in a parking lot for their beliefs. That's not activism. That's just you being an intolerable prick.

There's a Difference Between Having a Backbone and Being a Jackass.

Standing for something is admirable. But suppose your entire personality revolves around being an aggressive, obnoxious, virtue-signaling keyboard warrior who thrives on tearing people down. In that case, you might not be the savior you think you are. It's not strength. It's insecurity. Because strong people don't need to humiliate others to prove their point. Strong people don't need to scream the loudest to be heard. Strong people don't need to dehumanize the opposition to feel superior.

If your entire identity is based on being "against" something, but you have no idea how to engage with people in a non-combative way, congratulations, you're not a thought leader; you're just an angry internet troll with a cause. And that's precisely what they want.

The people in power love that we're too busy tearing each other apart to fix anything. Because while you're out here burning bridges with lifelong friends, disowning family members, and ruining relationships over a disagreement, the people at the top? They're laughing. Because guess what? They don't care about you. They don't care that you think you're fighting for them. They don't care that you think you're exposing the truth. They don't care that you feel your political rage is righteous. They care that you're distracted. Because as long as you're busy attacking the "other side," you're not paying attention to the game they're playing behind the scenes. They're still raising your taxes. They're still inflating the cost of living. They're still trading human rights like poker chips. They're still making backroom deals that screw all of us. And you're too busy yelling at strangers online to do something about it.

Hate is Profitable. The division is currency. The angrier we are at each other, the less we pay attention to them. The more we rip each other apart, the stronger their hold on us gets. And the best part? They don't even have to do the work anymore. Because we're doing it for them. We dehumanize our neighbors. We mock and belittle people we disagree with. We boycott family members over their political views. We treat opposing beliefs as mortal sins. And every time we do it, they win. They win when we see each other as enemies instead of people. They win when we refuse to listen and immediately resort to hate. They win when we throw away years of friendship over a disagreement instead of having a real conversation.

Meanwhile, the real issues that affect all of us? They stay the same. The people in power? Still untouchable. The cost of living? Still suffocating. The corruption? It's still running unchecked. The broken systems? Still benefiting the elite while screwing the rest of us.

What Now?

You can keep feeding the machine. You can keep being the exact kind of brainwashed, emotionally reactive puppet they want you to be. You can keep screaming at your neighbor while the people screwing you over count their money in peace. Or.

You can wake up.

You can choose to see people as more than just their political beliefs. You can start having honest conversations instead of just trying to "win" arguments. You can realize that humans are complicated, and morality isn't just a team jersey. You can stop falling for the divide-and-conquer tactics used to control people for centuries. Because? This isn't about politics. It's about how we treat each other. It's about whether we're going to keep falling for the same bullshit over and over again. It's about whether we will keep playing their game or start rewriting the rules.

And if your biggest takeaway from all of this is, "Well, yeah, but the OTHER side is worse!" well then, the rest of this book may be a challenging read....

The Illusion of Choosing a Side and Why No One Wins

Why do we have to pick sides? Are we not all on the same damn team? Do we not all want peace, happiness, freedom, and prosperity? Then why the hell can't we sit at the same table and work shit out? Politicians love to sell you lies. You're either with us or against us. You either support everything we do, or you're the enemy. You must pick a side and defend it at all costs. We'll take care of you.

Bullshit.

Life is not a binary choice. The world is not black and white. And yet, political parties, media, and social groups push the idea that if you're not 100% loyal, then you're a traitor. I'm sure some people avoid me because my politics don't agree with theirs. I sleep just fine. I get up to pee and return to sleep without their disgust of me crossing a single brain cell.

Supporting a party, a candidate, or a cause is excellent. But the second you stop questioning them and start unquestion-ingly defending everything they do, you've lost the plot. You have categorized your party's values over the actual lives of other people. Because guess what? Every side has its flaws.

Every party has corruption. Every politician is human with flaws, ambitions, and (often) a personal agenda (or disorder) that has nothing to do with helping you. And if you think your "side" is immune to that, my goodness, life will have surprises for you. The second you become so loyal to a political identity that you refuse to criticize it, you become easy to manipulate. Susceptible to suggestions. And guess who benefits from that? Not you.

How to Navigate Conversations Without Setting Your Brain on Fire

By now, you're probably thinking, "Okay, so what am I supposed to do? Just avoid politics forever?" No. But you do need to learn how to navigate these conversations without losing your damn mind or becoming the exact kind of rage-fueled, intolerable asshole you claim to despise.

Politics affect real lives. You can't just pretend they don't exist. But if your approach to politics involves shouting at people, alienating friends, and making enemies out of people you barely know, then you're not solving problems. You're just adding to the bullshit.

Stop Taking the Bait.

News outlets, social media, and politicians thrive on rage. Why? Because outrage is profitable. The angrier you are, the more you engage. The more you engage, the more money they make. If something is designed to make you angry first and think later, it's probably bullshit. If a headline feels like it was written specifically to piss you off, fact-check it before you

47

react.

Ask More Questions and Make Fewer Assumptions.

Instead of immediately attacking someone's belief, ask, "Why do you feel that way?" People's opinions come from somewhere. Their upbringing, their experiences, their fears. You don't have to agree, but you might learn their origins. You've already lost if you go into a conversation only to prove you're right.

Accept That You're Not Changing Anyone's Mind in a Facebook Comment.

No one has ever said, "Wow, this all-caps, condescending rant has truly changed my political views." If you want to influence people, be an example, not an asshole. People don't change their minds when embarrassed, mocked, or insulted. They change when they feel heard and understood and are given room to think. If you wouldn't say it to their face in real life, don't say it online.

Recognize When It's Time to Walk Away.

Some people don't want a conversation. They want an argument. They want to "win." If you find yourself in a debate where the other person is more interested in yelling than thinking, walk away. Your sanity is more valuable than "proving a point" to someone who isn't listening. Not every battle is worth fighting. Learn to spot lost causes and move on.

Remember That People Are More Than Their Politics.

Most people want the same things. Safety. Security. Opportunity. The ability to live their lives without fear. We disagree on how to get there. And that doesn't automatically make someone your enemy. If you can only define someone by who they voted for, that says more about you than it does about them. It might never have been that strong if you'd throw away a lifelong friendship over politics.

Things You Need to Accept About Politics

✔ People can have different views without being evil.
 ✔ You are not morally superior just because of how you vote.
 ✔ Your side isn't right about everything. Neither is theirs.
 ✔ Listening doesn't mean agreeing. It just means listening.
 ✔ Screaming louder doesn't make your argument better.
The Bottom Line?

If your political beliefs turn you into a bitter, angry, self-righteous person who alienates everyone around you, maybe the world is not the problem. Perhaps it's you. So, take a breath. Stop foaming at the mouth over every headline. Learn how to have a conversation instead of a battle. Because if we don't start talking to each other again, we'll never fix anything.

The world is not as divided as they want you to believe. Sure, people have different beliefs. Different opinions. Other ideas on how the world should work. But most of us aren't as far apart as we think. The real fight isn't between left and right. It's not between liberals and conservatives. It's not even between different political parties. The real battle is between those who want people divided and those who want people to wake up. So, the next time you find yourself getting sucked into political rage, ask yourself. Who benefits from this fight? If the answer isn't you, maybe it's time to stop playing.

4

CHAPTER 4: FAMILY—YOUR FIRST LESSON IN LOVE, LOYALTY, AND LOSING YOUR MIND

This may be hard to hear, but before society gets claws in you, politics tells you who to hate, and social media destroys your self-worth, your first taste of chaos comes from family. They are the people who shape us, break us, and result in us paying a few co-pays later in life. Family is supposed to be your safe place, your foundation, your ride-or-die squad. And for some people? It is. But for others? It's a hell you couldn't imagine.

Think about it: your family is where you learn everything about yourself and the world before you even know how to question it. Before you develop your voice. Before you understand choice. Before you realize some of the things they're teaching you might be completely wrong; they tell you who you are. They tell you how to behave. They tell you what to believe. They tell you how much of yourself you're allowed to show. They set the standard for love, acceptance, conflict, and survival. And if they screw it up? Well, congratulations.

You just won a lifetime subscription to unpacking your trauma with somebody like me.

Family Isn't Always the Warm, Fuzzy Hallmark Card

For some, family is safety. A place where they are loved unconditionally, where mistakes are learning moments, where their individuality is celebrated, not punished. For others? Family is fear. Walking on eggshells, never knowing what version of their parent or sibling they will get today. Family is control. A constant stream of, "We love you, but only if you do what we say, believe what we believe, and become what we expect." Family is conditional love. If you don't fit their mold or step outside their comfort zone, that love is suddenly held hostage. Family can be gaslighting. "That never happened." "You're too sensitive." "You're making a big deal out of nothing." Family is a battlefield. A place where words cut deep, fists fly, and silence suffocates.

The worst part? You don't even realize how much damage it's been doing for years, maybe decades. Because when you're raised in dysfunction, it doesn't feel like dysfunction. It feels like normal. It feels like home. So, when you finally step out into the world and see other families treating each other with respect, compassion, and understanding? It's like being told, "Hey, that fire you've been living in?" That's not actually what warmth is supposed to feel like." And suddenly, everything you thought you knew about love, safety, and identity? It crumbles.

The Lies We Tell Ourselves About Family

We grow up being told: "Family is everything." "Blood is thicker than water." "You should always forgive family." And on the surface, that sounds great, right? But let's talk about the full version of that "blood is thicker than water" quote.

"The blood of the covenant is thicker than the womb's water."

Translation?

The relationships you choose, the people who show up for you, respect you, and see you for who you are, are more important than those you were born into. Read that again. You do not owe loyalty to people who harm you just because you share DNA. You do not have to shrink yourself to fit into the version of you that makes them comfortable. You do not have to keep setting yourself on fire to keep your family warm.

Breaking the Cycle

If your family was your first source of chaos, your first experience of love mixed with pain, then at some point, you have a choice to make. You keep repeating the cycle, unconsciously passing down the same broken patterns. Or you break it.

And let's be clear: breaking the cycle is hard as hell. It means unlearning everything you were taught about love, trust, and self-worth. It means facing the uncomfortable truth that the people who raised you might have been wrong. It means healing wounds that aren't even yours to carry—but were handed down to you like a twisted family heirloom. And the most challenging part? It means choosing yourself, even when your family makes you feel like the villain for doing it. Because the moment you start setting boundaries, questioning old beliefs, and refusing to play the role they assigned you? You become the problem. "You've changed." "You're being dramatic." "You need to let the past go." "We're family; you're supposed to love us no matter what." **Love without respect isn't love.** If your family only loves you when you're quiet, obedient, and agreeable? That's not love. **That's control.** And if choosing your peace, truth, and happiness makes you the villain in their story? Then so be it because you're not responsible for upholding their version of reality.

You're responsible for creating your own.

Your Family is Like the First Software Installed on Your Brain

Have you ever gotten a brand-new phone with pre-installed apps you didn't ask for and can't delete?

That's your family. They download their beliefs, fears, expectations, and generational baggage into your system before you pick your first booger. By the time you're an adult, half your responses to life are just running on default settings you never agreed to.

Some families give you useful apps: self-worth, boundaries, and unconditional love. Others provide you with malware: guilt, control, and fear.

The bad part? You don't even realize some of that programming is toxic until you try to uninstall it. Because the moment you challenge the system, the system fights back. Try setting a boundary. You're selfish. Speak your truth? You're ungrateful. Express your emotions? You're dramatic. Want a different life than the one they expected from you? You're a disappointment.

Whether your family was supportive or straight-up dysfunctional, they shaped you. They gave you your first definition of love, respect, and boundaries (or the complete lack of them). They taught you what is "normal" before you even had the chance to ask, "But is it right?" And while some families build you up, others, intentionally or unintentionally, break you down.

So, if you've ever felt guilt-tripped, suffocated, controlled, or unworthy because of your family, it's not just you.

The Family Manual You Never Got

Let's be honest; some families operate like cults. Not in the robes-and-rituals way, but in the "You're either with us or against us" way. You're expected to follow the rules without questioning them. You're taught that family loyalty is more important than your happiness. You're guilted into forgiving, forgetting, and keeping quiet, even when hurt. You're told love is unconditional, but only if you play your role correctly. And the moment you step outside those lines? You become the problem. "Why are you bringing this up now?" "We don't talk about things like that." "You're being too sensitive." "That's just how we are." "You know how your [parent/sibling/relative] is; just ignore it."

You know what that is? Keeping peace at the expense of your own.

The Inheritance No One Talks About

Family doesn't just pass down genes. They pass down beliefs, fears, and generational wounds.

Maybe your family avoids conflict at all costs, so now you shut down instead of speaking up. Over-explains and over-apologizes, so now you constantly second-guess yourself. Believing success looks a certain way, so now you feel like you'll never measure up. It punishes emotional expression, so now you struggle to communicate your feelings. Using guilt as a weapon, so now you feel responsible for everyone else's happiness. And if you don't stop questioning it, you'll pass that programming on. If your family normalized emotional repression, you might think being vulnerable is weak. If your family relied on manipulation, you might feel guilt as love. If your family constantly shamed mistakes, you might think perfection is the only way to be accepted.

But here's what they didn't tell you. You do not have to carry what they handed you. You do not have to keep repeating patterns that never served you. You do not have to accept suffering because it's been passed down for generations.

Breaking Free From The Programming

If your family was your first source of chaos, healing is your rebellion. And unlearning their toxic patterns? That's better than a post-Thanksgiving shit! Except it's generational trauma hitting the bowl. Breaking the cycle means questioning the people you were taught never to question. It means choosing yourself, even when your family tries to make you feel like the villain. It means unlearning everything you were taught about love, safety, and identity and figuring it out for yourself. And sometimes? It means walking away.

This may hurt, but some family relationships can't be saved. Some people aren't interested in growth. Some people will never apologize. Some people would rather keep repeating the cycle than admit it's broken, and if holding onto them means losing yourself?

Let go.

Not with hate. Not with resentment. But with the understanding that you deserve better.

Loyalty Shouldn't Cost You Peace

We have this twisted idea that family comes first, no matter what. But love isn't unconditional if it comes with the expectation that you'll always be who they want you to be. If your family only loves you when you fit their mold... If your family only respects you when you agree with them... If your family only supports you when you don't make them uncomfortable... That's not family. That's control. And you don't owe anyone your silence, obedience, or suffering just because you share DNA.

Family isn't about blood.

It's about who gives a damn about your well-being.

Rewrite the Code

You are not a prisoner of your past. You are not doomed to repeat the same patterns. You can uninstall the bullshit your family downloaded into you. You can redefine love, safety, and respect for yourself. And if you have to burn bridges to build a better life?

Let them burn if necessary.

Because the family you create for yourself, built on respect, acceptance, and unconditional love, is worth more than the one you were born into.

The Difference Between Toxic Loyalty and Real Love

One of the most dangerous ideas about family is that "family is everything." Sounds nice, right? Until it's used as a weapon. Toxic families love to preach loyalty, but what they really mean is obedience. They expect you to ignore their bullshit, excuse their toxicity, and let them walk all over you because "we're family." Imagine you're at a restaurant, and the waiter keeps serving you spoiled food. The milk is chunky, the meat smells like it lost a fight with bacteria, and the bread has more mold than your college roommate's shower.

Imagine that whenever you refuse to eat, the waiter says, "But this is your grandmother's recipe! The family made this, so you HAVE to eat it!" That's how toxic families operate. They expect you to swallow whatever they serve, no matter how rotten, because "family is everything." But here's the truth: just because it came from your family doesn't mean it's good for you.

Here's the Hard Truth:

Real love supports you. It allows you to be yourself, even when it's uncomfortable. Toxic loyalty demands that you sacrifice yourself for the comfort of others. Real love respects your boundaries. Toxic loyalty calls you "selfish" for having any.

Real love lets you grow. Toxic loyalty shames you for changing.

If your family only "loves" you when you're doing what they want, that's not love; it's control. If you're only good enough when you shape your standards to meet theirs, that's not love; that's conditional care.

How to Set Boundaries Without Starting World War III at Thanksgiving

Ah, Boundaries. The magic word that sends controlling family members into a full-blown meltdown.

If you've ever tried setting a boundary with a toxic relative, you already know how this goes. You say, "I don't feel comfortable talking about that." They hear: "I'M PERSONALLY ATTACKING YOU." You say, "I can't make it to this event." They hear: "I HATE EVERYONE AND NEVER WANT TO SEE YOU AGAIN." You say, "I need some space." They hear: "YOU'RE A HORRIBLE PARENT AND I'M UNGRATEFUL."

Why does this happen? Because setting boundaries with family is hard, not because boundaries are unreasonable, but because they're used to having unlimited access to you. They've spent years, maybe decades, treating you like their personal emotional dumping ground, decision-making puppet, or unpaid therapist. And the second you start putting up guardrails, they act like you've committed a crime against the family. But guess what? You're Not Responsible for Their Reaction. Repeat it. You. Are. Not. Responsible. For. Their. Reaction. They can guilt-trip you. They can cry. They can call you selfish. They can throw a full-grown adult tantrum in the group chat. That's their problem. Your job isn't to make them happy at the expense of your peace. Your job isn't to bend backward so they can control you. Your job isn't to sacrifice your well-being so they don't have to confront their unhealthy behavior.

The Guilt-Tripping Olympics

Here's what they won't admit. If they truly loved and respected you, your boundaries wouldn't be a problem. But when you set a boundary, and someone immediately gets defensive? That's not love reacting. That's control panicking. And suddenly, the Guilt-Tripping Olympics begin.

The Emotional Extortion Routine

"After everything I've done for you..." "I guess I won't reach out anymore since you don't care." "One day, you'll regret treating me this way."

The Victim Performance

"Wow. I didn't know you hated me." "I must be the worst parent/sibling/grandparent ever." "I never thought you'd treat family like this."

The Reputation Smear Campaign

"They've changed. They don't care about family anymore." "They think they're too good for us now." "Their therapist is brainwashing them."

Notice something? None of these reactions respect your boundaries. They don't say, "I understand, and I'll try to improve." They don't say, "I may not get it, but I'll respect what you need." They don't say, "I'll work on that so we can have a healthier relationship." Instead, they flip the script so suddenly you feel like the bad guy. And that's the whole point. Because if they can make you feel guilty enough, you'll drop the boundary altogether.

Boundaries Are Not Betrayal

Here's where people get confused. Setting a boundary doesn't mean you don't love your family. It means you love yourself enough to stop tolerating bullshit. You can love someone and still say, "I won't allow this behavior." You can care about someone and still say, "I need space." You can value a relationship and say, "This dynamic needs to change." Love without boundaries isn't love. It's an obligation. It's performing the role of the "good" child, sibling, cousin, or grandkid—while silently resenting every interaction. And the truth is? Healthy relationships have boundaries.

If setting a boundary ruins a relationship, it means that the relationship was only functional when you had none. Write that down.

Sticking To Boundaries

Step one: Decide what you need. Do you need less contact or specific topics to be off-limits? Do you need to stop being their unpaid emotional punching bag?

Step two: Say it clearly. There are no lengthy explanations, no justifications. "I'm not comfortable discussing that." "I can't make it to that event." "I need space, and I hope you can respect that."

Step three: Brace yourself for the fallout. They will push back. They will test you. They will do everything in their power to make you fold.

Step four: Hold the line. No backtracking just because they're upset. No over-explaining to "make them understand." No caving to keep the peace.

People who respect you won't need to be convinced to treat you with respect.

If you have to beg, explain, or apologize for asking someone to treat you with basic human decency?

They never respected you in the first place.

The Freedom of Letting Go

You know what's funny? The moment you start setting boundaries, something incredible happens:

You start realizing how much weight you were carrying that was never yours to hold. The obligation to keep the family happy. The pressure to always say yes. The guilt that was never yours to carry. And once you let that go? You start breathing easier. You start reclaiming your time, your energy, your peace. You start seeing the people in your life for who they are—not just who they told you they were supposed to be. And sometimes? You start realizing that certain relationships weren't worth holding onto in the first place.

But most importantly?

You start choosing yourself. You don't owe anyone access to you just because you share DNA. Yes, family is essential. Yes, relationships take effort. But at the end of the day, is your family dynamic toxic, manipulative, or draining you?

You have every right to step away. Breaking free from toxic family patterns doesn't mean you don't love them. It means you finally love yourself enough to stop putting up with their bullshit. So, if you've been waiting for permission to put yourself first? Here it is because you deserve peace, even if it pisses some people off.

5

CHAPTER 5: FRIENDS— THE REAL ONES, THE SNAKES, AND THE WALKING RED FLAGS

Friends are the people you choose, unlike family, who you get stuck with by pure chance. Your friends are supposed to be your safe space, your partners-in-crime, your go-to when life sucker-punches you in the throat. But not all friendships are built to last. Some aren't good for you.

FRIENDSHIPS ARE NOT SUPPOSED TO HURT.

And yet they do. Yet, we let them.

I am not saying that friendships should be without challenge. The challenge is good. We can grow with challenge. We can learn from one another with challenges. But disrespect? Manipulation? Belittlement? Abuse? Your friends aren't supposed to treat you like a shopping cart. Use you when they need you, abandon you when they're done, push you recklessly, overload you, and leave you stranded in the parking lot like you were never valuable. Some friends lift you up, support you, call you out when you're screwing up, and push you to be better. Others? They drain the life out of you like an emotional mosquito, sucking you dry while convincing you that it's "just how friendship works." And the scariest part? Often, you don't even realize when a friendship has shifted from supportive to toxic. The same way clutter piles up in your car. At first, it's just a receipt, an empty cup, nothing major. Then, a few more things get tossed in, but you're busy, so you don't think about it. Before you know it, there's trash in the backseat, crumbs in the cup holders, and a weird smell you can't quite place. When you finally stop and look around, you're sitting in a mess that somehow became your normal. And the worst part? You don't even remember when it got this bad.

A Real Friend vs. A Toxic Friend

A real friend is someone who celebrates your wins without getting weird about it. Calls you out with love, not with passive-aggressive bullshit. Listens without waiting for their turn to talk. They want the best for you, not just when it is convenient for them.

A toxic friend is someone who guilt trips you when you need space or say no. Low-key (or high-key) gets bitter when you're doing well. They only show up when they need something. Makes you feel drained, unworthy, or anxious more than they make you feel happy. Sometimes, the people who say they have your back hold you back.

Why Friendships Don't Always Last (And That's Okay)

Friendship breakups hurt like hell. And nobody talks about them enough. Society romanticizes lifelong friendships as if you don't have a ride-or-die from elementary school; you've somehow failed at life. But the truth? People change. You change. Your priorities change. Your self-worth shifts. Your tolerance for bullshit changes. Your standards get higher. And sometimes, that means outgrowing people.

I learned that the hard way.

I have known a friend for nearly twenty years—TWENTY. That's longer than some marriages, longer than some people have been alive. Our history, good memories, inside jokes, and years of loyalty made me believe this was one of those forever friendships. Our families even talked about living on a compound someday.

But looking back? The signs were always there. The small jabs disguised as jokes. The way they always made their problems more significant than mine. The times I had to justify their shitty behavior to others and myself. But I ignored it because that's just how they are. Because they don't mean it that way. Because we've been friends forever. Because they have a lot going on.

I made excuses for their behavior. Hell, maybe they made excuses for mine.

Then, one day, it all came crashing down. And here's the best way I can describe it. It was like keeping an old, cracked phone charger. At first, it still kinda worked. You had to wiggle it a little, maybe hold it at a weird angle, but it got the job done. Then the wires started showing, and sometimes it wouldn't charge. But instead of throwing it out, you kept it. You told yourself, It's okay. I have to hold it a certain way. Until one day, sparks fly, it burns your hand, and you realize this isn't just unreliable. It's dangerous.

That's what it felt like when the friendship finally snapped. It wasn't just "Oh, we drifted apart." It was the realization that I had spent years twisting myself into weird shapes and stoking the narcissistic flames. I spent too long trying to drive a boat on train tracks rather than looking for water.

And the most challenging part? I let go of the person and the version of myself that tolerated it for so long. Friendships aren't always meant to last forever. And that's okay. Some people are only meant to be part of your story for a few chapters, not the whole book. You can still love them. You can still wish them all the happiness and success in the world. You can be grateful for every beautiful moment you share without sacrificing yourself to their toxicity. The thing is, they may even feel the same about you. Love each other. Grieve each other. But whatever you do, don't hold each other back.

Friendships are like shoes. Not every pair is meant for every mile. Some fit forever, and others wear out. You loved them once. They were comfortable, they carried you through some shit, they were your go-to. But now? They pinch. They hurt. They're falling apart. But instead of letting them go, you keep forcing them on, limping around in pain because you "should" keep them. That's how we treat some friendships. Just because someone was a good fit once doesn't mean they're a good fit forever.

The Vampire

We all know that one person—the one who only texts when they need a favor, the one who only reaches out when they are struggling but conveniently disappears when you need support. The one who treats your kindness like a subscription service, hitting you up when they need validation, advice, or help moving but vanishing the second you need something in return.

How do you know if someone is sucking you dry? Energetically, of course. They always talk about their problems but never ask about yours. When you need something, they're suddenly "so busy" or "going through a lot." They guilt-trip you when you say no. You feel obligated to answer their calls, even when you don't want to. You walk away from every interaction feeling drained.

Friendship is about give and take. But if you're doing all the giving and they're doing all the taking, that's not a friendship. That's a fucking vampire in disguise. And if you're feeling bad right now because you're realizing someone in your life fits this description? Good. That means you're waking up. It doesn't mean you must cut them off immediately (unless you want to). But it does mean you need to reassess how much access they have to you. Also, friends go through things just like we do. But understand this, you can support them in their struggles, and they can navigate their struggles without developing patterns of treating you like shit. You're not toilet paper, here to clean up the shit and get flushed.

Outgrowing People Doesn't Make You an Asshole

This is where we get stuck because we forget that sometimes, people suck. Because society drilled into us the idea that leaving people behind makes you a bad person. That "true friends" stick together no matter what. That cutting people off is "mean." If a relationship once mattered, you must keep nurturing it, even if it's toxic.

BUT. You don't owe anyone access because you have a history together. You are not obligated to keep people in your life if they drain you. You can love someone from a distance.

Sometimes, the kindest thing you can do for yourself and them is to walk away.

Hugging the Cactus

Returning to something that hurt you is like trying to hug a cactus because it used to be a lovely houseplant. Yeah, maybe once upon a time, it was small, harmless, and even cute. But now it's covered in spines, and every time you reach for it, you walk away bleeding. And yet, you keep going back, telling yourself, "Maybe this time it won't hurt." "Maybe they've changed." "Maybe if I approach them differently, it'll be okay."

But a cactus doesn't stop being a cactus just because you remember when it was soft.

And people don't automatically deserve another chance just because they were good to you once.

History Doesn't Equal Loyalty

We are obsessed with keeping people in our lives because they've always been there. Even if every time we see them, we feel smaller. "But we've been friends since childhood." "But they're family." "But they were there for me once." "But we used to be so close."

So what? People change. Relationships change. Not everyone is meant to go with you to the next chapter. Why are you still holding on if someone used to be good to you but is now toxic, draining, or manipulative? That's like saying, "Well, this milk was fresh when I bought it, so I should keep drinking it even though it's sour."

Sounds ridiculous, right?

So why do we do it with people?

Love Shouldn't Feel Like A Life Sentence

Just because you love someone doesn't mean you have to keep them in your life.

You can love someone and still walk away. Care about them and still set boundaries. Wish them well and still decide you're better off without them. Because love is not a life sentence. If the relationship is draining you, stressing you out, making you doubt yourself, or forcing you to betray your boundaries to keep the peace, it's time to let go.

The Fear of Letting Go

People cling to toxic relationships for the same reason they keep a dead houseplant—denial, guilt, and the irrational hope that it'll somehow come back to life. They're afraid of regret. "What if I miss them? What if I was wrong?" They're so scared of the unknown. "If I let them go, what if I don't find new friends? What if I end up alone?" They're afraid of looking like the bad guy. "They'll say I abandoned them."

Regret is temporary. Staying in a toxic relationship out of fear? That's a lifetime of suffering. You can survive the unknown. Being alone for a little while is better than being surrounded by people who make you feel lonely. You're not responsible for their narrative. People who mistreat you will always find a way to make you the villain. So smile for the camera.

Because choosing yourself doesn't make you a bad person; it makes you a person who values your peace.

How to Know It's Time to Let Go

How do you know if you're holding onto dead weight? Ask yourself: Do I feel worse after talking to them? Do I constantly have to explain or justify myself? Do they dismiss my feelings or make me feel guilty for having them? Do I dread seeing their name pop up on my phone? Am I the only one putting effort into this relationship? Would I want someone I love to be treated this way? If you're answering "yes" to most of these...

It's time to let go.

When Walking Away Feels Like Failure

If cutting someone off feels like giving up, remind yourself. You're not abandoning them. You're choosing yourself. You're not being cruel. You're protecting your peace. You're not breaking the relationship. It was already broken. You're just acknowledging it. And if they say: "You've changed." "You're being selfish." "You're making a mistake."

Remember, growth is a betrayal to those who refuse to grow with you.

Friendships Are Like Elevators—Some Take You Up, Some Keep You Stuck

Picture this: You're in an elevator. You press the button to go up. Some people ride with you. They grow, elevate, and celebrate the new floors you reach. But some? Some people want to stay on the same floor forever. And they expect you to stay with them. The second you try to level up, they start weighing you down, questioning your choices, guilt-tripping you, or resenting your growth.

You don't have to stay stuck just because they won't grow. If someone is holding you back instead of lifting you up, you're allowed to walk away. And no, you don't need a dramatic falling out. You don't have to burn bridges. You can slowly step back, stop reaching out, stop engaging, stop pouring energy into a friendship that's already run its course.

Some people will take it personally.

That's not your problem.

You are not required to stay small to make other people comfortable.

The Right Friends Don't Make You Shrink

The right friends add to your life. They don't drain you. They don't guilt-trip you. They don't make you feel like shit for having boundaries, needs, or a backbone. The right friends don't punish you for growing. They don't get offended when you change for the better. They don't view your success, happiness, or self-respect as a personal attack. And the more you start demanding that kind of friendship? The more you'll attract people who deserve a place in your life.

Friendship is a privilege, not a birthright. Just because someone was in your life for years doesn't mean they still deserve to be. Just because you used to be close doesn't mean you have to force a connection that no longer fits. Just because you love someone doesn't mean they're good for you, yet we hold on. We keep texting first, even when they never text back. We keep making excuses for their bad behavior. We keep pretending it's okay when they belittle, ignore, or take us for granted. Why? Because we were taught that loyalty is more important than self-respect. If a friendship was once good, we should keep watering it forever, even if it's already dead. But let me ask you something. When was the last time that friendship made you feel good? Not nostalgic. Not obligated. Not guilty of wanting more. Just...good.

If you have to beg someone to care, beg them to show up and match your effort—that's not a friendship; that's an unpaid emotional internship.

And you're working overtime for zero benefits.

73

Stop Watering Dead Plants

A friendship that no longer serves you is like a withered, lifeless plant. You can water it all you want. You can give it sunlight. You can hope and pray that it turns green again. But if the roots are rotten? If the is stem snapping? If life is gone? It's not coming back. And the longer you keep trying to revive it, the more energy you waste on something that doesn't want to grow. Meanwhile, there are real, healthy friendships out there, ones that don't make you feel exhausted. Ones that don't feel like a game of "prove your worth." But you'll never have the energy to build them if you're too busy pouring life into what's already wilted.

Stop Begging for Sunlight in Someone Else's Shade

You know what else sucks? Trying to thrive in a friendship where you're constantly being overshadowed. Where your needs always come second. Where your achievements are downplayed, where your feelings are brushed off, if you feel you have to dim yourself to keep a friendship alive, ask yourself: What are you getting out of it? Because real friends? They don't shrink you. They celebrate you. They support you. They remind you who the hell you are. And they sure as hell don't make you feel like you're asking for too much just because you want the same respect you give.

Give Your Energy to the Right People

The ones who show up, not when it's easy, but when it matters. The ones who make space for your feelings instead of dismissing them. The ones who don't see your boundaries as an inconvenience but as proof that you respect yourself. Because at the end of the day? Friendship is supposed to feel good. Not like a guilt trip. Not like an unpaid job. It's not like a one-sided effort where you're always the one trying. So do yourself a favor and let the dead friendships die.

Give your energy to the ones who care.

The ones who water you.

Let Go

Friendship should be a source of joy, not exhaustion. Audit them. Who makes you feel good? Who drains the life out of you? Who do you keep around out of guilt, not genuine connection? Start setting boundaries. Stop dropping everything for people who wouldn't do the same for you. Stop explaining yourself when you need space. Stop keeping people around out of obligation. Understand that friendships aren't about quantity. You don't need a massive friend group. A few solid people are worth more than a hundred fake ones. Let go of friendships that no longer serve you. Not with drama. Not with resentment. Just with the understanding that you deserve better.

6

CHAPTER 6: IDENTITY—WHO THE HELL ARE YOU (WITHOUT ALL THE NOISE)?

Society slaps labels on you before you even know how to speak. Before you could even say your name, the world had already decided who you were. They slapped labels on you like price tags at a yard sale. Your gender, race, family income, religion (or lack thereof), and a thousand other things that have nothing to do with who you are. And you? You just absorbed it. Because what else were you supposed to do? You were a blank slate handed a script before you learned to read. From the moment you took your first breath, the world started giving you a script you never agreed to but were expected to follow anyway. You were told what to believe, how to behave, and who to be before you even had the chance to figure it out for yourself. You were a boy, so you had to act like one. You were a girl, so you had to fit the mold. You belonged to a particular family, so you had to carry its expectations. You were part of a religion, so you had to accept its rules without question. You came from a specific background and had to stay within its limits.

No one asked you who you were. No one cared if the script made sense for you. You were supposed to play your part, hit your marks, and never ad-lib. But at some point, whether through pain, growth, or exhaustion, you start to wonder, what if I don't? What if you stop reciting the lines? What if you stop trying to be what everyone else decided you should be? What if you choose to be you instead? Because nobody asked for your input. They just told you who you were supposed to be. And if you ever dared to question it, that's where real problems started.

Because nothing pisses off society more than someone who refuses to fit into the box they were assigned.

Why Your Past, Your Job, or Your Relationships Don't Define You

The world loves to shrink people down into neat little categories. Your job? That's your worth. What is your relationship status? That's your identity. Your past mistakes? That's who you are forever.

Bullshit.

If your job, relationships, or past were the only things that made you "you," what happens when they disappear? If you lose your job, are you suddenly worthless? If you go through a breakup, does your identity vanish with the relationship? If you make mistakes, are you forever stuck as that person? Society conditions you to think your value is tied to something external, something they can measure, judge, or put in a category. Something they can point to and say, that's who you are. But who you are is not a resume. It's not a relationship status. It's not a list of regrets. It's you, the real you, beneath all the labels and the roles you play for others. And most people never get around to figuring out who that is. Because they're too busy trying to live up to someone else's idea of who they are. They are too busy shaping themselves into what's expected. They are too busy trying to fit into a box someone else built for them. They are too busy apologizing for what makes them different instead of owning them.

You don't owe this world a version of yourself that makes everyone else comfortable.

You owe yourself the chance to be fully, unapologetically, undeniably you—no permission required.

The Pressure to Be "Somebody" and Why That Definition is Rigged

Ever Feel Like You're Failing at Life Because You Haven't "Become Somebody" Yet? Spoiler alert: That's by design. From the second you start school, the pressure begins. Get good grades. Pick a career. Hustle hard. Make money. Get married. Have kids. Die. And at every stage, society whispers in your ear: "You're not enough yet. Keep going."

Here's the issue. There's no finish line.

Because even if you hit every milestone they set for you, they just move the damn goalposts. Got a degree? Cool, but do you have a good job? Did you land a good job? Nice, but when are you getting married? Got married? Cute, but when are you having kids? Had kids? Great, but why don't you own a house yet? Did you buy a home? Impressive, but when are you retiring?

It. Never. Ends.

The world keeps dangling a carrot of "success" in front of you, making you think you'll finally feel worthy when you reach it. But every time you get close, they yank it further away. That's why people hit their 30s, 40s, 50s, and beyond and still feel lost.

Because they spent their whole life chasing a definition of somebody that was never meant to be achievable, profitable, and palatable.

So, Who Are You?

That's the real question. If you stripped away every label, every expectation, every ounce of pressure, who would be left? Who are you when nobody is watching? What would you do if you weren't afraid of judgment? What makes you happy, not just accepted? For most people, the answer is:

I don't have a clue.

Because we've spent so long playing roles that we don't know how to be ourselves, we've been so conditioned to seek approval that we've forgotten how to exist outside of it. We can shift.

That's where you take back your power.

Because the second you stop trying to fit into someone else's expectations and start defining yourself for yourself, that's good shit.

How to Reclaim Your Identity (Without Losing Your Mind)

Question everything you were taught about who you "should" be. Where did your beliefs about yourself come from? Are they indeed yours, or were they spoon-fed to you since birth? Who benefits from you staying neatly inside the box you were placed in? Most of what you believe about yourself doesn't come from you. It came from parents, teachers, society, religion, and the media, each shaping your perception of who you "should" be before you ever had the chance to decide for yourself. You do have a choice. You can take a step back and challenge it all. You can ask yourself: Does this fit me, or am I just wearing a hand-me-down identity that was never mine? Rip off the labels. Rewrite the script. It's your life, so why the hell should someone else's expectations dictate who you get to be?

Stop Defining Yourself by External Shit

You are not your job. You are not your relationship status. You are not your mistakes.

Your worth was never tied to a paycheck, a last name, or a worst decision. But society sure as hell wants you to believe otherwise. From the moment you could comprehend words, the world drilled into you that your value was something external that could be measured, judged, and defined by how well you fit into their expectations. Your career, your achievements, your relationship status, your productivity, that's what they told you made you worthy.

Who you are exists outside of what you produce. Outside of the roles you play. Outside of how others perceive you. You were worthy before you ever did a damn thing. And you'll still be worthy long after the world stops keeping score.

Figure Out What Makes You Feel Alive

What excites you? What makes you feel free? What makes you forget to check your phone? Not what impresses people. Not what looks good on a résumé. Not what keeps you "safe" from judgment. What makes you feel something? And to clarify, if what makes you feel alive is harming other people, I highly recommend you consult with a mental health professional yesterday. There is no judgment, just urgency. Most people have no idea what fulfills them because they've spent their whole lives chasing what they were supposed to want. They followed the script, checked the boxes, and did all the "right" things, only to wake up one day wondering why they still felt empty.

I know this because I've seen it firsthand. I've sat across from people who had everything society told them would make them happy. They have money, titles, and achievements, yet feel entirely lost. I've talked to cops, veterans, and first responders who spent their entire lives in service to others, only to realize they had no idea who they were outside of the uniform. I've been in rooms with people on the edge, convinced their lives had no meaning because they couldn't see past their assigned roles. And I've watched the light flicker back into their eyes when they realized they weren't just their job, trauma, or mistakes. They were something more. They had passions, dreams, and desires buried under years of obligation and expectation.

And when they finally started peeling back the layers, when

they let themselves want things just because it made them feel alive, not because it was practical, impressive, or expected, you could see the shift. You could feel it.

That's what I want for you.

So, start there, not with what you should want, but with what lights you up. That's you. That's where you find the version of yourself who isn't just surviving but living.

Let Go of Who You Were "Supposed" to Be

You don't owe your past self anything. You don't owe society a neatly packaged version of you. You don't have to stay in roles that don't fit anymore. It's okay to change. It's OK to walk away. It's OK to say, this isn't me anymore.

Maybe you spent years trying to live up to expectations, yours, your family's, society's. Perhaps you made choices based on what felt right then, but it doesn't feel right anymore. Maybe you built an entire life around a version of yourself that no longer exists. And maybe, just maybe, that terrifies you.

That's normal. Change is uncomfortable. Letting go of the past, especially a past you put blood, sweat, and tears into, is hard. But you don't have to keep carrying the weight of a life that no longer fits just because you've been carrying it for a long time. You are not locked into any version of yourself just because it's the one people are familiar with. You're allowed to evolve. You're allowed to grow into someone different. You're not allowed to be the person other people expect you to be. And yeah, some people won't like it. Some will be confused. Some will try to remind you of who you "used to be" or guilt you into staying the same. But their comfort in who you were is not more important than your ability to become who you are meant to be. You only owe yourself the chance to be fully and freely you on your terms.

It's not the you that makes other people comfortable. Not the you that plays by the rules society handed you. The real you. The one who isn't afraid to grow, change, and step into the unknown. Because that's where you'll find freedom.

You Are Not for Sale

That's a weird thing to say, right? Imagine you're in an auction, and people keep throwing labels at you. "Smart." "Successful." "Attractive." "Hardworking." "A failure." "A mess." "Fat" "Ugly" (Insert any other dumb shit people label others with.)

And you keep grabbing the ones you think will get you the highest bid. Because that's what society teaches you. To become what's most valuable to others. To chase the labels that will make people like you, approve of you, choose you. But fuck that. Step out of the bidding war for approval. You are not for sale. You don't have to perform for approval. You don't have to mold yourself to fit someone else's " worthy idea." If the people eating at your table don't like the meal, they can starve!

The world has spent your entire life telling you who to be. Read that again. But now? You get to decide. So, stop asking for permission. Stop hunting validation from people who don't care. Stop outsourcing your self-worth to people who don't live your life. Rip off the labels. Burn the script. Write your own damn story.

Because the moment you realize their rules never bound you? That's when you start playing life on your terms.

7

CHAPTER 7: SOCIAL MEDIA—WHERE SELF-ESTEEM GOES TO DIE AND DELUSION THRIVES

In the bluntest way possible, I think social media is the worst thing that has happened to human civilization. Let's call it what it is. Social media is humanity's worst impulse control experiment, and we're all failing miserably. If aliens were watching us (which, honestly, I wouldn't blame them for avoiding), they wouldn't see a species advancing through technology. They'd see a bunch of over-caffeinated primates doom scrolling, arguing with strangers, and measuring their self-worth in emojis. Social media is a dumpster fire, but not the kind you can walk away from. It's the kind you sit around, staring at in horror, while someone throws gasoline on it every five seconds. And the worst part? We built this mess and then willingly shackled ourselves to it.

Why? Because the algorithm told us to.

How the Algorithm Profits From Your Insecurity

Let's start with a brutal truth: social media was never designed to make you happy. It wasn't built to connect you. It wasn't made to keep you informed. It wasn't even created to help you express yourself. It was built to keep you addicted, and what's the easiest way to do that? Make you feel like absolute shit about yourself, so you keep coming back for validation. Think about it. When was the last time you closed a social media app and thought, wow, I feel so much better about my life!? Exactly.

Social media thrives on your insecurity because insecure people are easy to manipulate. And guess what? If you feel ugly, you'll click on beauty ads. If you think you're unpopular, you'll chase engagement. If you feel behind in life, you'll compare yourself to strangers. If you feel angry, you'll argue in the comments. And every single one of those emotions = profit. More insecurity → More scrolling. More scrolling → More ads. More ads → More money for the people running this shit show.

So, yeah. The game is rigged, and you're the product.

It's like a casino that only takes your dignity as currency. The house always wins, and the jackpot is your self-esteem in shambles.

Fake Authenticity—Why Everyone's Full of Shit Online

Have you ever seen someone post a raw, vulnerable, totally real post... that happens to have perfect lighting, flawless makeup, and a deep, meaningful caption that sounds suspiciously like it was work-shopped in a focus group? Yeah. That's the problem. Fake authenticity is everywhere. It's influencers crying on camera right after adjusting their ring light for the perfect tear-streaked glow. It's celebrities posting "no makeup, just me" selfies... with five filters and an entire glam team behind the scenes. People perform relatability not because they want to be accurate but because being authentic is trending. And the wildest part? Even the people who are full of shit online are ALSO comparing themselves to other people who are full of shit online. It's like a bunch of mannequins having a self-esteem crisis over which one looks the most lifelike.

This isn't just about influencers and celebrities. Regular people like you and me get sucked into this mess too. We crop, edit, and filter our lives to look just untidy enough to be relatable but not so dirty that it makes people uncomfortable. We post our "bad days," but only those that are still aesthetically pleasing. We share our struggles, but only those we've already overcome because nobody wants to admit they're still in the middle of the storm. Why? Because we've been conditioned to package everything for consumption. Even our pain. Even our most human moments. And let's be fundamental: authenticity should not require this much effort. If you have to curate it, think hard about how to make your vulnerability palatable; guess what? It's not real.

Genuine authenticity isn't found in the perfectly captioned

post about struggle. It's a mess. The unfiltered, unpolished, awkward, "I have no idea what the hell I'm doing" moments that never make it to the highlight reel. So maybe the real challenge isn't just spotting fake authenticity; it's unlearning the idea that we need to package our lives for public approval in the first place. Because the most fundamental thing you can do is stop trying so hard to look actual and just be.

Doom Scrolling & Outrage Culture

Ever hop on social media for "just a second" and suddenly realize you've lost an hour doom-scrolling through lousy news, angry posts, and videos that somehow made you feel worse about humanity? Or how about the absolute truth? None of us are pooping for forty-nine minutes. We handle business in five and spend the following forty-four watching videos of other people watching videos of other people while our legs turn to TV static. And our spine bends to a degree incompatible with upright mobility.

That's not an accident. Social media thrives on negativity because outrage = engagement. Anger gets more comments. Controversy gets more shares. Division keeps you coming back for more. The algorithm isn't built to give you essential news; it's built to provide you with engaging news. Which means the loudest, angriest, most dramatic bullshit always rises to the top. Why? Because when people fight in the comments, they stay on the platform longer. And when they stay longer, they see more ads. And when they see more ads?

More profit.

At this point, social media isn't even a conversation; it's a rage-powered slot machine, and every time you pull the lever, your aunt is telling you they will pray for your evil words, your uncle is mad about the immigrants, Johny quarterback from high school is now an astrophysicist with a GED, and the local conspiracy theorist is tracking the elusive unicorn elf queen of Northern Illinois. Don't look it up. It's not real. Or is it?

How to Exist on Social Media Without Letting It Screw With Your Self-Worth

Now, I'm not about to tell you to quit social media altogether.

It's 2025. Quitting social media is social exile at this point because, hell, do people even go outside anymore? But you can learn to use it without letting it use you.

Unfollow Anyone Who Makes You Feel Like Shit.

Yes, even that "friend" you keep hate-following to roll your eyes at their posts. Unfollow toxic people. Mute accounts that trigger comparison. Block anyone who drains your energy.

Your feed is like your mental diet; if it's full of junk, your brain is going to feel like garbage.

Stop Using Social Media as a Measure of Self-Worth.

Social media numbers are nonsense. How many likes did I get? Did they watch my story? Why didn't they comment? Who gives a shit? They are watching your videos while they poop.

Remember That Most People Are Lying (Even If They Don't Mean To).

That perfect couple posting "so in love" pictures? It might not be perfect behind the scenes. Is that influencer bragging about their ideal life? They might be faking it for engagement. That person who always looks flawless? Spent 6 hours preparing for that video.

Take a Damn Break.

Ever notice how much clearer your head feels after spending time away from social media? Delete the app for a day, turn off notifications, and go outside without your phone. If the idea of doing that makes you panic... guess what? That means you need to do it. Dopamine comes in many forms, not just from a screen.

Use Social Media Intentionally—Not as a Mindless Escape.

Almost every single one of us does this. Scrolling out of boredom, anxiety, or habit. That's how the algorithm digs its claws into your brain, feeding you just enough dopamine to keep you hooked but not enough to satisfy you. It's a never-ending loop of compare, crave, consume, repeat, designed to keep you chasing a version of life that isn't even real.

Next time you open an app, ask yourself. Do I want to be here right now? Is this adding value to my life? Or am I just filling time? Social media isn't evil. But it is a carefully designed system built to exploit your insecurities, steal your time, and

89

keep you addicted.

So, keep mindlessly scrolling, letting social media screw with your head, your time, and your self-worth. Or. Take back control, and use social media on your terms, not theirs. Because at the end of the day? You should be running your life, not an algorithm.

Now, as my wife would say, go and touch a tree.

The Danger of Social Media Giving Everyone a Platform

I am a proud supporter of every breathing human having a voice and a right to free speech; however, some people should not have a platform to speak to the masses. Seriously, imagine if social media existed in the 1930s and 40s. There was a time when you only had a few options to be entertained and informed. Now? Any rando with WiFi and a spicy opinion can broadcast their thoughts to millions. And spoiler alert: Most have no idea what the hell they're talking about. But we click on their bullshit anyways.

Social media didn't just give everyone a voice; it gave megaphones to the room's loudest, least informed, and most unhinged voices. And the algorithm? Oh, it loves them. Because guess what generates the most engagement? Misinformation. Conspiracy theories. Manufactured outrage. Random dudes with zero credentials are making bold claims in their cars. Remember when knowledge came from experts? Now, it comes from "alpha male mindset" TikToks, Twitter threads from high school dropouts who swear they've cracked the code to the universe, and Facebook moms pushing essential oils to cure everything.

The dumbest voices often drown out the smartest ones. Why? Because the algorithm rewards engagement, not accuracy. It doesn't care if something is true; it cares if it gets clicks. That's why a doctor with 15 years of experience gets ignored while Chad, who read half an article once, makes viral medical claims. We've reached a point where being loud is more valuable than being right, where hot takes are more profitable than facts, where expertise has been replaced with confidence. The result? A world where bad ideas spread faster than ever, where outrage mobs form over misinformation, and where actual progress gets buried under the sheer weight of bullshit. So next time you see a viral post making wild claims, ask yourself. Does this person know what the hell they're talking about? Or did the algorithm decide they should be famous for the day?

Just because someone has a platform... doesn't mean they should, especially if lies pay their bills.

8

CHAPTER 8: BELIEFS—YOUR BRAIN'S OPERATING SYSTEM

Every one of us has beliefs—ideas we wrap around our hearts with the hope they're true. But I have bad news for you. Just because you believe something is true doesn't mean it is. AND THAT'S OKAY! Do you ever stop and wonder why you believe what you believe? No, seriously. Take a second. Why do you think certain things are right and others are wrong? Why do you have strong opinions about some stuff and zero cares to give about others? Why do you feel guilty for thinking differently than how you were raised? Why does questioning something feel like committing mental treason? Because your brain has been programmed. Not in some Matrix-level sci-fi way (although that would explain a lot), but in a very real, psychological way. Your beliefs are the operating system running your life, and guess what? Most of them weren't even installed by you.

We've talked about it. A massive chunk of the things you "know" to be true was shoved into your mental hard drive by other people—your parents, your culture, your teachers, your religion, your government, your society, your childhood experiences, the media you consumed, and even that one friend in middle school who convinced you that stepping on a crack really would break your mom's back. Seriously, didn't you think quicksand would be a bigger problem? Grow any watermelons in your belly after eating a seed? It's programming. Some harmless. Some harmful.

Some of it is outdated. Some of it was installed with a virus called fear. And some of it? Some of it was designed to keep you controllable, obedient, and too scared to ask questions.

But you can update your operating system. You can download new software. You can question, reprogram, and rebuild your beliefs into something that works for you instead of against you.

Let's start hacking your brain.

Where Your Beliefs Come From: It Ain't Just You

Your beliefs aren't some pristine, original thoughts you handcrafted in a philosophical vacuum. Nope. They're a Frankenstein monster of influence, fear, and repetition. And it starts way earlier than you think.

Family: The First Programmers

Before you could walk, talk, or decide whether you like pineapple on pizza, your family was already downloading their beliefs into your tiny brain. "This is good, that is bad." "This is how we do things." "People like us believe this." And you didn't question it. Why would you? The people feeding you and keeping you alive must know what's best, right? And if you

93

ever did question it, you were probably met with: "Because I said so." "That's just how the world works." "Don't ask questions." And just like that, your first batch of beliefs got installed without your permission.

Society: The Factory Settings

Once you step out into the world, society takes over. And oh boy, does it have some strong opinions about who you should be, how you should act, and what you should believe. Schools push certain narratives. Religion lays down rules. The news tells you what to fear. Social media warps reality. And if you start questioning any of it? You get labeled. Question tradition? You're disrespectful. Challenge authority? You're a troublemaker. Think differently? You're crazy. Notice a pattern? Society doesn't like free thinkers. It likes obedient participants.

Fear: The Ultimate Manipulator

If you want to control someone, you don't need force; you need fear.

Keeps people in line. Fear makes people cling to beliefs, even if they don't make sense. Fear convinces people that questioning something will lead to chaos, suffering, or punishment. "If you don't believe in this, bad things will happen." "If you go against this, you'll be rejected." "If you change your mind, you'll regret it." Ever wonder why certain beliefs are so hard to shake? Because they're tangled up with fear. Fear of being wrong, fear of losing your identity, fear of not knowing what the hell to believe anymore.

Faith. The Software Running Your System

Let's talk about faith. Religion. Spirituality. The stuff that shapes entire cultures, builds communities, sparks wars, and defines personal identities. It's woven into history, politics, and how people make sense of their existence. It's the big one. The topic that makes people shift in their seats, lower their voices, and choose their words carefully. The one people tiptoe around because nobody wants to be seen as the "bad guy" questioning something sacred. After all, faith is personal. It's deep. It's tied to who we are, where we come from, and sometimes what we fear.

But faith shouldn't be fragile. If a belief system falls apart the moment it's questioned, was it ever that strong? If a belief can only survive by demanding absolute, unquestioning loyalty, is it faith or fear? Genuine faith, whatever form it takes, should withstand scrutiny. It should hold up under pressure, adapt, evolve, and stand firm not because it's forced to but because it's built on something real.

So, let's talk about it without fear, guilt, or the need to pretend we have all the answers. Because if faith is the software running your system, wouldn't you want to know exactly what's in the code?

Why You Believe What You Believe

If you were born in India, you'd probably be Hindu. If you were born in Iraq, you'd probably be Muslim. If you were born in Italy, you'd probably be Catholic. If you were born in the middle of nowhere with no exposure to religion at all, you might never think about it. See the pattern?

Like everything else, faith is downloaded into you before you know what it means. Your family's faith becomes your faith. Your culture's practices become your practices. Your community's beliefs become your moral compass. And for many people, that's where the questioning stops because asking, "Why do I believe this?" feels like a betrayal. If you were raised with a religious background, questioning your faith probably felt like: "If I ask this, I'm doubting everything." "If I don't believe exactly what I was taught, I'm turning my back on my family." "If I explore something new, I'm wrong, or worse, doomed." Faith is meant to be explored, not unthinkingly followed.

Religion vs. Faith. They're Not The Same.

Most people confuse faith with religion. But faith? That's personal. That's your relationship with whatever higher power you do or don't believe in. Religion? That's the structure. The rules, traditions, rituals, and interpretations were created and passed down over centuries. And while faith can be deeply personal, religion is often used as a tool to control, manipulate, and enforce conformity. Faith says, "Love your neighbor." Religion says, "But only if they fit our criteria." Faith says, "Seek truth." Religion says, "But only the truth we approve of." Faith says, "Your journey is between you and the divine." Religion says, "You must follow these exact steps, or else." At its best, faith brings peace, connection, and purpose. At its worst? It's weaponized and used to hurt people, to be correct.

But let's talk about the good because true faith can heal, uplift, and transform despite how religion has been twisted. Faith gives people the strength to get through their darkest days when stripped of ego, fear, and control. It's what has pulled people back from the edge and given hope where there was none.

I've seen faith in its purest form when people, broken and lost, find something to hold onto that keeps them breathing one more day. After witnessing the worst of humanity, I've seen it in law enforcement officers who still believe in something bigger than themselves. I've seen it in people who have lost everything but still wake up and choose kindness.

Faith, genuine faith, isn't about control. It's about connection to something greater, to each other, to hope itself. Authentic faith doesn't rob others of the hope it seeks.

When Faith Becomes Fear.

Religion, in its purest form, is supposed to be about guidance. A moral compass. A way to understand the world and find comfort in chaos. But the second fear gets involved? It turns into control. "If you don't believe this, you'll suffer." "If you question this, you're a sinner." "If you don't follow this exactly, you're doomed." And suddenly, faith stops being about connection and starts being about compliance.

Why do so many people hold onto religious beliefs they don't resonate with? Fear is a robust leash. People stay in spiritual communities that make them miserable because they're afraid of losing their family, their support system, and their entire world. People follow rules they disagree with because they've been told questioning them is dangerous. People bury doubts because admitting them out loud might mean rejection.

But chew on this.

If your faith is only strong because you're afraid to question it, is it faith or conditioning?

Faith Evolves.

This may sound like the craziest thing you've ever heard, but you can evolve spiritually. Your relationship with faith is not a static, one-time decision. Your understanding of the divine can grow, shift, and expand. Your beliefs can change as you gain wisdom, experience, and new perspectives because no one has all the answers. Not your parents. Not your religious leaders.

Not the books written thousands of years ago. Not that guy on Twitter who thinks he's got it all figured out. And not me. And that's a good thing. The moment you stop questioning, exploring, and seeking, faith stops being faith and starts being a cage. Real faith? It moves with you. It grows as you grow. It shifts when you learn more, experience more, and become more. Whether you believe in God, the universe, energy, or just the power of human connection, faith, in its most accurate form, is about finding peace in the chaos and holding onto something that makes life worth living.

What To Do If You Are Questioning Your Beliefs

First of all. Good. Beliefs are meant to be questioned, and if you believe your maker's skin is so thin that you can't question outcomes and life's absurdities, how can you expect them to have the answers you seek? If your God is real, they can handle your questions. Doubt isn't a weakness. It's a sign that your brain is working. So, explore it instead of fighting it, fearing it, or shoving it down.

Separate Faith From Fear

Ask yourself: Do I believe this because I genuinely feel connected to it? Or do I think it is because I'm afraid not to?
Because faith shouldn't feel like a cage. Does your belief
system only exist because of fear, obligation, or pressure? It
might be time to rethink it.

Question Everything (Yes, Everything)

Genuine faith can handle questions. So go ahead, ask them.
What do I believe is separate from what I was taught? Do I
agree with the moral framework of my religion, or accept it
because I was raised with it? Would I still follow the same path
if I weren't afraid of judgment? And if asking those questions
scares you? That's even more reason to ask them.

Permit Yourself to Evolve

Faith isn't about having all the answers. It's about being open
to discovery. Maybe you stay in your faith, but in a way that
feels more aligned. Perhaps you find a different path that fits
your soul better. Maybe you realize you don't need religion to
be a good person. Whatever your journey looks like, it's yours.
   No one else gets to dictate it.

Believe In Something That Makes You Better: Not Smaller

Does your belief system lift you up, make you kinder, give you
peace, and encourage growth? Beautiful. Hold onto that. But
if your belief system shames you, controls you, makes you

afraid to question, or turns you against others? Maybe it's time to update your software. Because at the end of the day, faith should set you free. Not keep you in chains. And if loving people, genuinely loving them, without conditions, without judgment, without treating them like a problem to be fixed, sends us to hell?

Then I guess that's just the dice we rolled.

I don't know about you, but I'd rather stand for love and be wrong than stand for fear and be right. I'd rather live with an open heart than a closed mind. I'd instead choose kindness over conformity. Because if the price of being a decent human being is eternal damnation, then maybe, just maybe, the system is broken. And I refuse to spend my life shrinking myself, hating people, or living in fear just to fit inside a box someone else built.

So, believe in something that makes you better, not smaller.

Believe in something that brings you closer to others walking the same confusing journey as you.

Believe in something that makes you want to love people. **Not change them.**

And let the dice fall where they may.

Belief And Truth Are Not Synonymous

This might hurt. Belief doesn't always equate to truth. Belief is just a thought you keep thinking, while truth exists whether you believe it or not. But here's where people get stuck: They confuse what they think with what is true. "I believe I'm not good enough." → NOT a truth. Just a shitty belief someone or something planted in your head. "I am capable of learning, growing, and improving." → Truth. No belief is required. "I believe anyone who disagrees with me is wrong." → That's just arrogance wrapped in certainty. "Different people have different perspectives." → Truth. The danger comes when people get so attached to their beliefs that they refuse to update them, even when faced with new evidence.

If you want to evolve, if you're going to grow, you have to learn how to open the damn door. Imagine this. It's 2025, and we've got satellites orbiting the planet, live streaming from space, and an overwhelming amount of scientific evidence proving the Earth is round. Like. People are up there. Looking at it. Right now. And yet, people are still convinced that our planet is as flat as a pancake. P.S. I ain't arguing with you, so don't @ me. Or tweet me. Or X me. Or whatever the damn thing is called now.

How can we believe something that has been proven wrong? Because our beliefs become a mental cage.

Flat-earthers, for example, have built their entire identity around the idea that they've uncovered the "truth", that they're more intelligent than the "sheep" who believe in a round Earth. No matter how much undeniable proof is shoved in their face, they refuse to update their belief. Why? Because changing their mind would mean admitting they were wrong. It would mean undoing years of arguing, conspiracy theorizing, and maybe even rebuilding their worldview. And for some people? That's too much to handle. Don't be mad, flat-earthers. We can all live together in harmony.

So, instead of evolving, they double down. They twist logic into pretzels to defend their belief. They dismiss facts, attack experts, and convince themselves that any evidence contradicting them is fake news. This is what happens when belief overrides the truth. It's not about reality anymore;

it's about identity. And that's the real danger. When your beliefs become so sacred, changing your mind feels like losing yourself.

The way out? Humility. Curiosity. Willingness to evolve. If your beliefs can't change and they won't adapt even when reality smacks them, then they're not beliefs anymore.

They're a prison.

And the only way forward is to open the damn door.

How To Challenge And Evolve Your Beliefs Without An Existential Crisis

Updating your beliefs isn't about throwing everything you know into the trash and starting from scratch. It's about doing a quality check on the shit that's running your life.

Identify the Beliefs That Might Be Bullshit

Ask yourself: Where did this belief come from? (Did I choose it, or was it given to me?) Who benefits from me believing this? (Does this belief empower me or keep me small?) Is this belief true, or is it just familiar? If a belief isn't serving you, not allowing you to grow, or based on fear instead of truth, it might be time to let it go.

Challenge It Like a Scientist

This may shock you, but science and theology can coexist. When scientists test a theory, they don't just unquestioningly accept it. They question it, test it, and look at the data. So, do the same with your beliefs. Is there actual evidence for this, or just feelings? Have I ever questioned this or just accepted it? Do I still believe this, or am I just afraid to stop? And if a belief doesn't hold up under scrutiny?

Replace It With Something Better

Letting go of an old belief can be scary because it leaves a gap in your mental framework. But that gap is also an opportunity to install something better. So instead of: "I have to believe what my family believes." "I get to decide what makes sense for me." "If I change my beliefs, people will judge me." "If people can't handle my growth, that's their problem." "I have to be certain about everything." "I'm allowed to question, learn, and evolve."

Your beliefs shape your reality. They affect your self-worth, your choices, your happiness. So, shouldn't you make sure they serve you? You don't have to believe everything you were taught. You are allowed to change your mind. You are not obligated to hold onto beliefs that make you miserable. And if questioning your beliefs makes people uncomfortable? Well, maybe it's because they haven't updated theirs yet. So go ahead. Hack your brain. Run the update.

Believe what you believe and do so strongly.

But beliefs shouldn't hurt people.

Including you.

9

CHAPTER 9: FACTS VS. OPINIONS – WHY EVERYONE THINKS THEY'RE RIGHT

Welcome to the age of everyone's an expert and the internet bullshit buffet. A guy with a YouTube channel and zero credentials can convince millions that tiny fairies fly up their nose while they're sleeping, but a scientist says the earth is getting hotter, and people shout FAKE NEWS!

Explain. No, seriously, explain.

People believe anything with a catchy headline; no fact-checking is required. Everyone thinks they're experts, even when they don't know anything. Once upon a time, expertise required, well... expertise. Years of study. Real-world experience. Maybe even a little thing called evidence.

But now? Who needs facts when you can feel like you're right? Who needs research when you can find a TikTok that agrees with you? Who needs logic when you can scream louder than the other person and declare victory? It's a mess. A chaotic, brain-melting, shit-warming mess. And the worst part?

It's contagious.

The Internet Doesn't Reward Truth: It Rewards Noise And Outrage

Misinformation spreads faster than the flu at a daycare. And most people aren't even stopping to ask, "Is this true?" before hitting "share." Why? Because the internet isn't built for truth. It's built for engagement. And what gets engagement? Clickbait. Outrage. Dumbed-down, oversimplified nonsense.

It doesn't matter if it's true. It just matters if it gets clicks. Thoughtful, nuanced discussions? Boring. Facts backed by research? Yawn. Taking the time to consider both sides? Who has the patience?

Instead. "This ONE SHOCKING FACT will change EVERY-THING you thought you knew!" "Scientists HATE him!" "The media is LYING to you!"

And suddenly, we've got a world of people who think reading one meme makes them more informed than experts.

Why Everyone Thinks They're Right

Here's a fun fact: Your brain loves being right. It loves it so much that it actively ignores information that proves it wrong. Your brain clings to being right like a raccoon with a stolen donut, so obsessed with holding onto it that it'll ignore every sign that it's rotten, moldy, or not even a damn donut.

It's called confirmation bias. And it's the reason flat earthers dismiss satellite images. Anti-vaxxers ignore scientific studies. Conspiracy theorists believe "the real truth" is always the thing that sounds the most dramatic. Because once you feel something, your brain starts filtering reality to protect that belief. It doesn't matter if the belief is wrong. It doesn't matter if evidence exists to prove otherwise. It doesn't even matter if the belief is entirely ridiculous. Your brain will prioritize whatever information supports it and reject everything else. That's why arguing with someone deep in a belief system (no matter how absurd) feels impossible. Because they're not just defending an idea. They're protecting their entire identity.

Why People Are Addicted To Misinformation

Because the truth is complicated, and complicated doesn't go viral. The internet is built on SPEED. The faster a message spreads, the more power it has. And what spreads fast? Simple answers to complex problems. Bold claims with no proof. Anything that triggers an emotional reaction.

Which of these is more likely to go viral? A: "The economy is affected by a wide range of complex factors, including global trade policies, labor markets, and fiscal regulations." B: "IT'S THE GOVERNMENT'S FAULT. WAKE UP, SHEEPLE."

Exactly. People don't want to think. They want to feel like they already know. This is why misinformation isn't just an accident; it's a business model. It's why politicians use fearmongering instead of actual solutions. It's why influencers push half-baked theories that sound smart but collapse under scrutiny. It's why companies spend millions on ads convincing you that their product will change your life, even if it's just a bottle of overpriced vitamins.

Because logic doesn't sell, emotion does.

When someone becomes emotionally invested in an idea,

they will fight tooth and nail to defend it, even when it's wrong.

When Opinions Dress Up As Facts For Halloween

Another reason misinformation spreads? People think "I feel like this is true" is the same as "This is true." Spoiler alert: It's not. "I feel like the news is lying, so they must be." "I feel like climate change isn't real, so it's not." "I feel like the election was rigged, so that's the reality." Your feelings are real. That doesn't mean your conclusions are. The world doesn't bend to our emotions. The Earth isn't flat just because some guy on the internet says NASA is part of a global conspiracy. Vaccines don't stop working just because your cousin's best friend's dog groomer heard a scary rumor. Science doesn't care how much you "just feel like" something is fishy. Reality exists outside of personal perception. But when people confuse belief with fact, they stop looking for truth. They stop asking questions. They stop learning. They stop growing. And suddenly, the loudest voices in the room don't know the most.

They're just the ones who refuse to admit they might be wrong.

Staying Sane In A Misinformed World

So, how do you survive in this chaos? How do you keep your head while everyone else is screaming nonsense?

Question Everything (Yes, Even Yourself)

Where did I get this information? Is there actual evidence for it, or does it just sound good? Am I believing this because it's true or because I want it to be true?

Slow Down

The next time something outrageous pops up on your feed, pause. Does it make sense or make you mad? If it's designed to trigger you, it's probably intended to manipulate you.

Accept That You're Not Always Right

I know. The news is shocking. How will the world continue spinning if it learns you didn't know everything? I have news for you. The greatest scientific minds in existence, the Sir Isaac Newtons of the world, don't know everything. They know a whole lot of shit about a whole lot of shit, but they don't know everything. I consider myself intelligent, especially in areas of the brain, human behavior, law enforcement, and stress management. However, I ain't scared to admit that I am an absolute dumbass in most other areas of life. That's wisdom. Knowing you're equally intelligent and capable of being wrong. Being wrong isn't a weakness, nor does it mean you aren't smart. It just means that you were wrong about something for 8 seconds of your life. It's okay to be a silly little human. The strongest people are the ones who can say, "I was wrong, and now I know better." You're probably not thinking critically enough if you haven't changed your mind about anything important in the last five years.

108

Stop Giving Loud, Ignorant People Your Energy

Maybe just let ignorant people be ignorant. Not every battle is worth fighting. Some people don't seek the truth; they want to argue. Let them yell. Go live your life.

The Internet Turned Everyone Into An Expert

There was a time when if you needed to know something, you went to an actual expert, someone who studied the topic for years, someone with credentials, someone with actual, provable knowledge. Now? Karen from Facebook read one WebMD article and suddenly knows more about vaccines than epidemiologists with decades of experience. Some guy Googled 'how planes fly' for two minutes and now believes he can land a 747 in an emergency. Bill, who barely passed high school chemistry, is explaining how Big Pharma is hiding the cure for cancer in a Facebook rant. A guy who watched two conspiracy videos on Facebook suddenly thinks he knows more than scientists, doctors, and historians combined. "I don't trust experts." "I did my research." "I know the truth because I saw a TikTok about it."

Fun fact: Watching a 90-second video does not make you an expert. It makes you someone who watched a 90-second video. But here's the problem: It makes people feel like an expert. And when someone feels they know something, they're less likely to question it.

This produces my biggest pet peeve on the planet: the Dunning-Kruger Effect, a psychological phenomenon in which people who know little about something overestimate their knowledge. In contrast, well-informed people question themselves more (because they understand how complex things are).

Translation: The loudest, most confident people in debates often know the least, while the quiet ones who understand the topic are out here doubting themselves because they know how much there is to learn. That's why the internet is a dumpster fire. It doesn't reward people who say, "I don't know enough about this topic to have a strong opinion." It rewards people who say, "I AM RIGHT, YOU ARE WRONG, AND HERE'S A SCARY HEADLINE TO PROVE IT!" That's how misinformation thrives.

Remember: You can't convince an idiot with fifty facts, but you can convince fifty scholars with one truth.

How Misinformation Spreads

Here's a wild statistic: Fake news spreads six times faster than real news. Why? Because truth is often tedious, complex, or inconvenient, but bullshit is spicy. Consider it: "Experts say climate change is real and caused by humans." It's complicated, requires effort to understand, and is kinda depressing. "A secret cabal of billionaires is using HAARP machines to control the weather and flood your town on purpose." Exciting, dramatic, explains why things suck in a way that makes people feel special for knowing "the truth."

Guess which one goes viral? The internet loves simplicity and emotion—and misinformation checks both boxes. It gives people someone to blame (which feels good). It confirms what they already believe (which feels even better). Understanding requires zero effort (which means lazy people eat it up). It's not about truth anymore; it's about ego. This is why conspiracy theories, political lies, and viral nonsense spread like wildfire. It's easier to believe something outrageous than it is to accept reality. It's more fun to share a dramatic claim than to fact-check it. It's more comfortable to agree with your side than to admit maybe you were wrong.

This is why the world is a what the fuck sandwich.

Emotional Reactions vs. Actual Logic

You're not as logical as you think. Everyone loves to think they're rational, critical thinkers. "I only believe in facts." "I'm not biased." "I think critically." No. No, you don't. Your brain isn't a cold, calculating machine that sifts through data with perfect precision. It's a cluttered, emotional, impulse-driven chaos engine. And unless you actively train yourself to separate emotion from logic, you're just another emotional creature pretending to be rational.

The Emotional Hijack: How Your Brain Lies to You

The human brain is wired for emotion first and logic second, and this isn't just some motivational poster nonsense. It's hardwired neuroscience.

Your brain has two key players in decision-making:

The Limbic System (Your Emotional Brain)

This is the ancient part of your brain responsible for survival. It reacts first, fast, and without much thought. Fear, anger, excitement, disgust? They are all limbic systems. It doesn't care about facts; it just cares about immediate emotional

111

responses.

The Prefrontal Cortex (Your Logical Brain)

This is the newer, more evolved part of your brain. It handles reasoning, logic, and critical thinking. The problem? It works slower than the emotional brain. By the time your logical brain starts analyzing, your emotional brain has already formed an opinion, and now, it's working backward to justify it.

How This Plays Out in Real Life

Here's how the average person processes information online. You see something that pisses you off. (Example: A headline that says, "Scientists Say Coffee Causes Cancer.") Your emotional brain kicks in immediately. ("Oh hell no. I drink coffee every day. These 'scientists' are full of shit.") You immediately believe it's false because it feels wrong. ("I've been drinking coffee for years and am fine! More fake news.") You share the post with an angry comment before fact-checking. ("More lies from the so-called experts! Drink coffee, people!") Boom. The cycle continues. The logical brain never even had a chance to do its job.

Why Feelings Are Mistaken for Facts

Strong feelings are not the same as strong evidence, but your brain often treats them identically. The stronger your emotional reaction to something, the more accurate it feels. The more it aligns with your beliefs, the more you assume it must be correct. The more it scares you, the more urgently you share it without stopping to verify if it's real. And that's why we live in a world where facts get ignored if they don't feel good.

The Power of Emotion Over Evidence

A scientist presents peer-reviewed data proving vaccines save lives. A random dude says, "My cousin got sick after a shot, so I KNOW they're dangerous!" Who do people believe? The random dude. Why? Because a personal story is emotional. Data is boring. Statistics might tell you that 99.99% of vaccinated people are OK. But that one dramatic story of a bad reaction? That sticks. It triggers fear. It feels true.

This is why people believe in scary headlines over well-researched articles. A viral TikTok rant feels more convincing than a doctor explaining the science. Conspiracy theories spread faster than the boring truth.

Learning How to Think Critically

If you want to survive without turning into another rage-fueled, misinformation-spreading zombie, you must start thinking critically. Here's how.

Assume You Might Be Wrong

The moment you start believing you're always right, you stop learning. Stay open. Stay curious. The most intelligent people ask questions, not just shout answers.

Fact-Check Before You Share

If you see something that makes you emotional, stop and check if it's true. Rule of thumb: If it pisses you off, there's a high chance it was designed to manipulate you.

Recognize the Difference Between Feelings and Facts

Feelings: "This makes me mad, so it must be true!" Facts: "Let me check the data before forming an opinion." One of these makes you a critical thinker. The other makes you part of the problem.

Avoid Echo Chambers

If everyone around you thinks exactly like you, you're probably trapped in an echo chamber. Challenge yourself. Talk to different people. Seek out perspectives you disagree with.

If Someone Screams, They've Already Lost

The second someone resorts to yelling, insulting, or dismissing you, they don't have a solid argument.

Facts don't need volume; they stand on their own.

The Emotional Brain vs. The Logical Brain: How to Flip the Switch

When you're emotional, your amygdala (the part of the brain responsible for fear, anger, and emotional reactions) takes over. This leads to knee-jerk reactions, impulsive decisions, and falling for misinformation designed to provoke you. But here's the trick: You can manually switch from your emotional brain to your logical brain (the prefrontal cortex) by doing something straightforward:

ASK YOURSELF A QUESTION.

That's it. One simple question can pull you out of the emotional spiral and force your brain to engage logic. Try these. Is this true, or does it just confirm what I already believe? What would I think if the roles were reversed? What's the counterargument to this? Where's the evidence?

Why does this work? When you ask a question, your brain has to pause, analyze, and search for an answer, instantly shifting activity away from the emotional brain and into the logical one.

It's like pressing the brakes on a speeding car before you crash into a wall of bullshit. We're living in an era where bullshit travels faster than facts, where everyone thinks they're right, and where critical thinking is treated like an inconvenience. You can either keep getting manipulated by emotions, misinformation, and whatever garbage gets thrown at you online. Or. Start thinking for yourself. The choice is yours.

But if you're gonna argue, at least bring receipts.

10

CHAPTER 10: CULTURE—THE UNWRITTEN RULES THAT SHAPE YOUR REALITY

Culture is the invisible hand that shapes you. The unseen force that molds how you see yourself, others, and how you move through the world without realizing it. It's the silent architect of your thoughts, the unspoken rulebook you've been following since birth, the script you didn't get to write. It decides what's "normal," what's "acceptable," and what makes you "worthy." And here's the kicker: Most of it? It's complete bullshit.

From the moment you take your first breath, culture starts programming you. It hands you a blueprint for your life before you even know what life is. It tells you what to believe, how to behave, who to respect, who to fear, what success looks like, and what failure means.

And you're expected to follow along, no questions asked. The programming is subtle, sneaky, and often disguised as "tradition," "values," or "just the way things are." It's passed down like an old, dusty playbook that nobody bothers to rewrite.

Culture is both a guide and a trap.

It can be beautiful. It can connect you to something bigger than yourself, give you a sense of belonging, and create community. It can give meaning to your existence, remind you where you came from, and help you navigate the chaos of life. But it can also limit you. It can control you. It can keep you small. It can tell you who you're allowed to be and punish you for stepping outside the lines. It can convince you that your worth is conditional and that you must earn love, respect, and validation by following someone else's script.

So, the question isn't, "Does culture shape you?" Because it does. It always has. The real question is:

Are you shaping it back?

The Subconscious Ways Culture Programs How We See Ourselves and Others

Let's play a little game.

Think about the first time you felt ashamed of something about yourself. Judged someone for being different. Decided what "success" looked like. You thought, "People like me don't do that." It felt like you weren't enough. Now ask yourself: Where did that come from? Did you wake up one day and decide to think that way? Or did it get implanted in your brain before you even had a chance to question it?

Culture is sneaky like that. It programs us in ways we don't even recognize. And by the time you're old enough to think

117

critically, the damage is already done. You've been trained, without even realizing it, to see the world through a specific lens.

All right, imagine your brain is like a blank canvas. Fresh, untouched, full of potential. But before you even pick up a brush, other people start painting on it. At first, it's just little strokes, "This is good," "That's bad," "People like us do this," "People like them do that." You don't question it because, well, you're a kid. You don't even realize the painting is happening.

Then, one day, you step back and look at the whole thing. And you realize it's not even your art. It's a jumbled collage of other people's opinions, society's rules, expectations, fears, and biases, all slapped onto your canvas before you ever had a say. Now, the real question is: Do you keep letting others paint over your life, or do you grab the damn brush and make it your own?

It Tells You What's "Beautiful"

Thin, but not too thin. Curvy, but only in the right places. Dark skin? Lighten it. Pale skin? Tan it. Too much makeup? You're fake. No makeup? You're lazy. Short hair? Not feminine enough. Long hair? Too basic. Too sexy? You're "asking for it." Not sexy enough? You're invisible. No matter what you do, someone will tell you you're wrong.

It Tells You What's "Successful"

Go to school. Get a degree. Get a "real" job. Get married. Buy a house. Have kids. Retire. Die. If you follow the checklist, you're a good citizen. If you don't? You're lost, failing, or wasting your potential.

It Tells You Who To Respect, And Who To Dismiss

Certain professions are considered worthy of admiration, while others are looked down on. Some people's voices automatically carry more weight than others—not because they're more intelligent or capable, but because of their gender, race, class, or background.

It Tells You Who To Fear

Ever notice how some groups of people are constantly painted as "threats"? How specific communities villainized, stereo-typed, and treated as dangerous before they've even said a word? That's not random. It's by design. And if you don't question it, you'll absorb it without realizing it.

It Tells You Who You're "Allowed" To Love

Who you should marry. What kind of relationships count? What kind of love is acceptable? And if you step outside the box? Be prepared for judgment, rejection, or worse.

It Tells You What To Believe

It hands you a prepackaged set of morals and values, wrapped up in the idea that this, and only this, is the "right" way to live. That questioning the script makes you rebellious, dangerous, or wrong. And just like that, you're molded into something that fits within the system. You learn to play by the rules, even if those rules don't serve you. You learn to measure your worth by standards you never agreed to. You learn to stay in line because stepping out of it has consequences. And unless you actively challenge it, you'll spend your life playing by rules you never wrote.

The Difference Between Respecting Tradition and Being Trapped By It

Tradition can be beautiful. It connects people across generations, gives meaning to life, and creates shared experiences. But not all traditions are worth keeping. The problem isn't tradition itself; it's when tradition becomes a prison. There's a fine line between honoring and being trapped by the past. Does a tradition bring people together, strengthen relationships, or add joy to life? Keep it. Does a tradition require suffering, shame, or obedience? Question it. If a tradition excludes, discriminates, or forces people into roles they never chose? Burn that shit to the ground.

Think about the traditions you follow. Are they meaningful to you? Or do you do them out of guilt, obligation, or fear of judgment? Because the truth is, just because something has been done for a long time doesn't mean it's right. "But that's how we've always done it." Yeah? We always believed the Earth was flat, too, which didn't hold up very well. Flat earthers are going to hate me. It's okay, guys; I still love you.

Every significant change in history started with someone questioning the rules.

Rosa Parks & The Bus Boycott

Society told her, "People like you sit in the back." She said, "No, I don't." And that one moment of defiance lit the spark for the Civil Rights Movement. The rule was there, but that didn't mean it was right.

Galileo & The Church vs. Science

Back in the day, the Catholic Church swore that Earth was the center of the universe. Galileo dared to look through a telescope and say, "Uh... actually, no." He got labeled a heretic for it, but guess what? He was right.

The Suffragettes & Women's Right to Vote

Women were told for centuries, "You're not built for politics. Voting is a man's job." Susan B. Anthony and a legion of badass women said, "Screw that." They protested, got arrested, and changed the law to give women a voice.

Alan Turing & Breaking the Enigma Code

Society said, "War is won with brute force." Turing, a gay man at a time when being gay was illegal, said, "Actually, how about math?" He built the first modern computer, cracked Nazi codes, and shortened WWII by years, saving millions of lives.

Jackie Robinson & Breaking the Color Barrier in Baseball

Baseball was white only. That was the "rule." Jackie Robinson stepped onto the field, took all the hate and abuse thrown at him, and proved he wasn't just good; he was legendary. Now, every MLB team honors his number, 42, every year.

Harvey Milk & LGBTQ+ Rights

The world told him, "Stay quiet, stay in the shadows." He became the first openly gay elected official in California and fought for LGBTQ+ rights until the day he was assassinated. His legacy still impacts laws today.

Malala Yousafzai & Girls' Education

The Taliban told her, "Girls don't need an education." She got shot in the head for saying, "Yes, we do." Instead of backing down, she became the youngest Nobel Prize winner in history, fighting for girls' education worldwide.

These people weren't superheroes. They weren't born immune to fear, doubt, or society's expectations. They just looked at the world and refused to accept a bullshit status quo. And that's the thing: every significant change in history started with someone questioning the rules. Someone who realized that just because a belief is common doesn't mean it's right.

The people who challenged gender roles, racial segregation, oppressive laws, religious hypocrisy, and outdated norms? They weren't "disrespecting tradition." They were freeing people from it. And if you find yourself feeling trapped by the expectations of your culture, here's your permission slip to let that shit go.

How to Unlearn Toxic Cultural Expectations

Do you ever realize you've been following a rule your whole life... and then suddenly wonder why that rule even exists? That's the first step to unlearning cultural programming and recognizing it. Ask yourself: "Who benefits from this?" Who benefits from you hating your body? Who benefits from you working yourself into exhaustion? Who benefits from you staying silent instead of speaking up? Who benefits from you feeling like you're never enough?

Spoiler: It's usually people in power.

Stop giving a damn about "what people will think." Most of the shit you're afraid of, judgment, rejection, disapproval, isn't actually about you. It's about other people's programming. And guess what? They're gonna judge you no matter what. So do you anyway.

Challenge every "should." "I should get married by now." Says who? "I should look like this." Who made that rule? "I should have my life figured out." Yeah, no one does. Every "should" is a rule someone made up. And you don't have to follow it.

Replace guilt with choice. Guilt is the number one tool culture uses to keep you in line. Instead of feeling guilty for breaking a rule, remember: I choose what works for me.

Surround yourself with people who think freely. Do you ever notice how some people expand your thinking while others reinforce the same old bullshit? Seek out the ones who make you question, grow, and rethink.

Unlearning cultural conditioning isn't about rebelling for the sake of rebelling. It's about reclaiming your mind. It's about choosing who you are instead of letting culture decide for you.

Why Representation Matters More Than Most People Think

Did you grow up watching movies, reading books, or flipping through magazines where no one looked like you? No one shared your experience? No one made you feel seen? I didn't have that problem. I grew up as a white kid in Appalachia America. Every show and movie I watched growing up had white people in it. I remember being surprised whenever I saw a person of color on television. If you can't see a problem with that, especially up to this point in the book, maybe you've reached your final page. But before you go, I encourage you to watch little Black girls reacting to the new Little Mermaid that looks like them. It's beautiful. It's also society's fault that they must feel surprised when they see someone who looks like them. I hope in a few hundred years, we are all just a big, blended group of people who don't care about who's different.

For decades, media and culture have been controlled by a small, influential group of people who decide what "normal" looks like. And if you don't fit their "normal" version, you're either erased, sidelined, or misrepresented. And that matters. Because when you don't see yourself reflected in the world around you, it sends a message, a quiet but relentless whisper in the back of your mind: You don't belong. You don't matter. You are not the default. And even if no one says it out loud, you feel it.

If you're a woman and every "strong leader" in history books is a man? You internalize that. It plants the idea, consciously or not, that power, leadership, and intelligence belong to men while women's contributions are footnotes at best. If you're LGBTQ+ and every movie either ignores or stereotypes your identity? You internalize that. You start to believe that your existence must be mocked, erased, or treated as a side plot, never the main story. If you're a person of color and the only time people who look like you are on screen is when they're criminals, sidekicks, or struggling? You internalize that. It warps how the world sees you and, worse, how you see yourself. If you're disabled and every show, every ad, every piece of media acts like people like you don't exist? You internalize that. And when you are represented, it's often through an outdated, pity-filled narrative that reinforces the idea that disability means being less than others. If you don't fit into rigid beauty standards and only the people celebrated as "attractive" look the same, you internalize that. And before you even realize it, you start measuring your worth against an impossible standard you were never meant to fit.

This isn't just about movies, books, or media; it's about the subconscious programming that starts early and shapes how we view the world and our place in it. And the effects are real. When people don't see themselves represented, they start shrinking themselves. They second-guess their dreams. They question whether they deserve to take up space. And when representation does exist but is always negative, it teaches the world to see them through a distorted lens, one that leads to real-world consequences like bias, discrimination, and systemic inequality.

Representation isn't about checking a box or being "politically correct." It's about showing people that they exist. That they matter. Their experiences are real, their stories are valuable, and they are just as worthy as anyone else. It's about ensuring the next generation knows they belong instead of questioning it. So, the next time someone says, "Who cares about representation?" The answer is simple:

Anyone who has ever felt invisible. **Any. Fucking. One.**

Not just the one looking back at you in the mirror.

Culture will shape you whether you like it or not.

But now? Now, you get to decide what to keep, what to reject, and what to rewrite. If a belief serves you, keep it. If a rule limits you, break it. If a tradition feels wrong, change it. Culture shouldn't tell you who to be. It should enhance what you already are.

You don't have to be a prisoner to someone else's version of life.

You get to write your own damn story.

II

PART II: WELCOME TO THE STRUGGLE SHOW

Seeing the world for what it is was the first step; now comes the hard part. This section dives into the fight between who you've been and who you're becoming. Struggle isn't a sign of failure; it's proof that you're in the process of breaking free. We'll tackle self-doubt, fear, and the battles that keep you stuck. Growth is uncomfortable, but so is staying the same. The question is: are you willing to push through the struggle to find something better?

11

CHAPTER 11: WELCOME TO THE STRUGGLE SHOW

This part? This is where shit gets real. This is where we stop pretending that the chaos of the world is something we can scroll past, joke about, or compartmentalize. This is where we talk about how much of it has seeped into you, shaping how you think, move, and doubt yourself before breathing. Society didn't just throw chaos at you; it programmed it into you. From the moment you could understand words, you were handed a script. A script about who to be, how to act, what to fear, and what to believe. And now? You're left sorting through the mess, trying to figure out which parts are genuinely you and which were installed without your permission. And listen, this part might sting. It might rip open wounds you've barely had time to acknowledge and bring up memories you've shoved so far down they feel like another lifetime. But let me be clear: I am not here to hurt you. No words in this book exist to attack, shame, or judge you. They exist to wake you up. To give you a fighting chance. To remind you that your life is yours to reclaim without the weight of every expectation, every lie, every piece of conditioning that was never meant to serve you.

Because someone once gave me something that changed everything: a moment of clarity. An opportunity to challenge the poison in my mind. To realize that the world hadn't just happened to me; it had shaped me, manipulated me, and convinced me that my limitations were fundamental when, in fact, they were manufactured. And I want to hand that moment to you now. So, may I share?

Suppose the first half of this book was about exposing the external chaos, the dumpster fire of society, the bullshit systems designed to keep you small, and the unspoken rules created to control you. Then this half? This is about the war that happens inside you because of it—recognizing that the world is a mess. That's easy. Admitting how much of that mess has shaped you, broken you, and convinced you to doubt yourself? That's the real battle. How much of it has dictated your self-worth? How much of it has made you question your voice? How much of it still echoes in your head late at night, whispering the same old doubts, the same old fears, making you wonder if you're okay or just really good at pretending.

But here's the truth they don't want you to know: You don't have to accept every thought that enters your mind. You don't have to believe everything you were told growing up. And you sure as hell don't have to carry pain that was never yours to hold. This is where we take it back. Your thoughts. Your beliefs. Your power.

The world has spent your entire life telling you who you are, how you should feel, and what you should believe.

Now? You get to decide.

The Battle You Didn't Enlist For

This isn't the feel-good, motivational, "just think positive!" bullshit that self-help books love to sell you. This is the part where we examine the fundamental, raw, uncomfortable truths about Loss. Trauma. Mental health. Identity. Self-worth. The parts of life that gut you. That change you. That leaves scars.

Because whether you realize it or not, you've been in a fight your entire life. A fight against grief. A battle against shame. A fight against fear. A fight against every voice, external or internal, that ever told you weren't good enough.

It's time to stop fighting yourself and start fighting for yourself.

The Voices In Your Head Aren't Always Yours

I'm not saying you have schizophrenia. You might. But I'm talking about a different kind of voice. Have you ever noticed that the shitty things you believe about yourself don't even sound like you? That voice that says: "You're not good enough." "You're too much." "You're unlovable." "You'll never get better." Where did that come from? A parent who only showed you love when you were "perfect"? A teacher who made you feel like you'd never measure up? A religion that said you were broken just for being human? A society that profits from your insecurities?

Not every thought in your head belongs to you. Some of them? They were installed. By fear. By conditioning. By people who benefited from your self-doubt. And now, those voices live in your head rent-free, whispering doubts whenever you try to step into your power.

But what if I told you... you don't have to listen anymore?

Trauma Rewires, It Doesn't Define

Trauma isn't just a struggle; it's a relentless force. Not the kind you joke about, not the kind you can shake off. It burrows deep, rewiring your mind and reshaping your reality in ways you never signed up for. I've seen firsthand what trauma does. It follows you into the quiet moments, silences you when you need to speak, and closes your eyes to the good that still exists. It's exhausting. It steals pieces of you, tricks you into thinking it's your identity, and convinces you that healing is out of reach. But here's what I've also learned: trauma doesn't get the final word.

It doesn't just leave memories. It doesn't just hurt in the moment. It rewires your brain. It sneaks into the way you think, the way you react, the way you expect the world to be. Trauma doesn't just show up when you think about the past; it lingers in your present, whispering lies about your worth, safety, and future.

It teaches you things that aren't true, that love is dangerous, that people always leave, and that you must be on guard 24/7 because the worst is always around the corner. And even when the danger is gone, and you're safe, your brain doesn't get the memo. It still holds onto it like a bad habit, like a broken alarm system that won't shut off, like a warning light that stays on even when the engine is fine. It's why you flinch at love, even when it's real. You expect abandonment, even when no one's leaving. You struggle to trust, even when no one's lying. You feel like happiness isn't meant for you, even when it's right in front of you.

Because trauma isn't just what happened to you; it's how your brain learned to survive it. But hear me when I say this: your trauma is a chapter, not the whole book. Yes, it left scars. Yes, it changed how you see the world. Yes, it still echoes in your mind when things get quiet.

But it does not get to define the rest of your story unless you let it.

The Choice You Didn't Know You Had

Let's shift right here. This is where you realize you have a choice. You can keep believing the lies. You can keep letting the past rob you of every enjoyable thing in front of your face. You can keep fighting battles that were never yours to begin with. You can look your past in the eye and say, "I have the power. Not you!" You don't have to keep believing what they told you. You don't have to keep carrying pain that isn't yours. You don't have to let the worst moments of your life define who you are. You get to unlearn. You get to rewrite. You get to heal. Not because it's easy. Not because it happens overnight. But because you deserve to be free.

You are NOT what happened to you. You ARE what you do with it. It won't be easy. But it'll be worth it.

The Mental Massacre Ends When You Stop Fighting Yourself

When you stop fighting yourself, your body, and your mind give you permission to heal, and trauma waves the white flag. Your brain realizes it doesn't have to protect you from your past. Then, it starts helping you build a future with the lessons you've learned, the insights you've gained, and the strength you've summoned. This isn't about pretending the pain isn't real. This isn't about slapping a motivational quote on your suffering and calling it healing. This isn't about ignoring the past and forcing yourself to "move on." This is about taking back the power you didn't know you had. The power to challenge the bullshit you were taught. The power to rewrite the beliefs that keep you stuck. The power to stop treating yourself like the enemy.

Because you were never meant to fight against yourself.

You were meant to fight for yourself.

You're worth saving. Invest.

The Battles You Never Signed Up For

Nobody asks to be hurt. Nobody asks for loss. Nobody asks for trauma, anxiety, depression, self-doubt, or the constant exhaustion of trying to prove they deserve to exist. But life doesn't care about what you asked for. It throws the worst at you without warning, mercy, or a pause button to catch your breath. And when it does? You don't get to bargain with it. You don't get to return the pain like a defective product. You have to carry it, whether you're ready or not.

Grief? It doesn't show up with a warning label or a handbook.

It just rips someone you love away and leaves you standing there, staring at the wreckage, while the rest of the world keeps moving like nothing happened. Like they didn't just vanish from your life, leaving behind empty rooms, missed calls that'll never be answered, and memories that used to be warm but now feel like knives.

And the worst part? People expect you to "heal." To "move on." To somehow function as if you're not waking up every morning with a hole in your chest that nothing can fill. They tell you time makes it better, but they don't tell you that time makes it different. The pain doesn't shrink—you learn how to carry it without breaking in half.

Trauma? It rewires your brain, makes you flinch at things that shouldn't scare you, and convinces you that normal people's things, trust, love, and safety, are risks instead of rights. It turns your mind into enemy territory, where a sound, a smell, a sentence can transport you back to the worst moment of your life, and no one else even notices. People who haven't lived it will tell you to "just let it go," as if trauma is some heavy bag you're carrying instead of something that's stitched into your skin as if you wouldn't drop it in a heartbeat if it were that easy.

Mental health struggles? They make you feel trapped inside your own body, watching everyone else live while you try to figure out if you're still in control of yourself. It's not just sadness. It's not just stress. It's like drowning in an ocean that looks calm from the outside while everyone around you keeps asking why you don't just stand up and walk to shore. Some days, you can fake it. You smile, nod, and say, "I'm fine," because it's easier than explaining a battle no one else can see. Other days? You barely have the energy to exist, let alone pretend. But the world doesn't slow down just because you're fighting a war in your mind.

And self-worth? Oh, that's the trickiest one of all. Because self-worth isn't just about how you see yourself, it's about every message you've ever absorbed from the world telling you what you're "supposed" to be. It's about the impossible standards, the expectations you never agreed to, the silent rules that say you have to earn your place, your voice, your right to take up space. You were never supposed to believe you were enough as you are. The world profits from your insecurity, from your need to be thinner, stronger, more prosperous, more successful, more likable, more of whatever they're selling today.

But here's the thing: You don't have to play that game. You don't have to spend your life trying to be "enough" for people who were never supposed to have a say in your worth in the first place. You don't have to measure your value in productivity, appearance, or whether or not people approve of you. These are the fights nobody prepares you for—the wars nobody teaches you how to win. And yet, here you are.

Still breathing.

Still here.

Still fighting, whether you realize it or not.

That means something, even when it doesn't feel like it.

The World Wants You to Get Over It—But That's Not How This Works

Ever notice how people get uncomfortable when you talk about real shit? Grief, trauma, depression, these things don't fit into the neat little timelines society tries to slap on them. You don't get three to five business days to process your pain and then walk it off like a minor inconvenience. But that's precisely what the world expects from you. "You have to move on." (Move on to what? My entire reality just changed. You think I can swap out my pain like a pair of worn-out shoes?) "You should be over it by now." (By whose fucking timeline? Yours? Society's? The grief police? Am I supposed to set a calendar reminder for when my feelings are officially inconvenient for you?) "Other people have it worse." (Oh, so because someone else is drowning, I should pretend I'm not sinking? Pain isn't a competition.)

Here's the truth: You don't just 'get over' shit that breaks you. You learn to live with it. And no, that doesn't mean ignoring it, numbing it, or pretending you're fine when you're not. It doesn't mean slapping on a fake smile because the world would rather you be digestible than honest. It means sitting with the pain, even when it's ugly or makes other people uncomfortable. Even when you wish you could fast-forward through it. It means acknowledging that what happened to you mattered. It means understanding that healing isn't a straight line; it's a messy, chaotic, unpredictable process without a deadline.

It means making peace with the fact that some wounds don't heal perfectly, but that doesn't mean they must keep you bleeding forever. This section of the book? It's not about "fixing" you. You were never broken to begin with. It's about facing the parts of yourself you've been avoiding. It's about unpacking the weight you've been carrying. It's about taking back the power that pain tried to steal from you.

Because at the end of the day, the only way out of this fight... is through it. And no one gets to tell you how long that takes.

The Lies You've Been Told About Strength

Let's talk about the word "strong" for a second. People love telling you to "stay strong" when going through hell. They throw it at you like it's some magical shield that'll protect you from feeling pain. But what do they mean when they say it? Most of the time, "stay strong" is just code for "stay silent." "Don't make us uncomfortable with your pain." "Don't cry where we can see you." "Don't fall apart in a way that inconveniences the rest of us."

Screw that.

Strength is not pretending you're okay when you're not. It's not forcing yourself to be "fine" so other people don't have to deal with the messiness of your emotions. It's not bottling up everything you feel because you were taught that vulnerability is a weakness somewhere along the way.

Real strength? It's looking your pain dead in the eye and refusing to let it own you. It's grieving, fully and unapologetically, even when the world tells you to hurry up and get over it. It's acknowledging your trauma without letting it become your whole identity. It's understanding that what happened to you matters, but it does not get to define you.

Strength is knowing that asking for help doesn't make you weak. That struggling alone isn't noble; it's just unnecessary suffering. Strength is breaking down when you need to, knowing that tears aren't a sign of failure; they're a sign that you're still feeling, healing, processing, and human.

You are not weak for feeling things deeply. You are not weak for breaking down. You are not weak for needing time, space, support, or even just a dang break. You are human. And if you're still standing, no matter how shaky it feels, still pushing forward despite everything that has tried to take you down?

That's strength. That's resilience. That's survival.

Nothing can take that away from you unless you let it.

Welcome to the Fight for Yourself

This part of the book is going to be heavy. It's going to be uncomfortable. It might even piss you off. Good. That means it's working. Because healing? It's not passive. It's not soft. It's not something that happens while you sit around waiting for time to do the work for you. Healing is a full-blown battle. It's an all-out war between you and the things that have tried to break you. And if you're expecting it to be easy, you're in for a rude awakening. It's not easy to get back up when the weight of the world tells you to stay down. It's not easy to unlearn the lies you've been fed about what it means to be strong. It's difficult to fight for yourself when you've spent years believing you weren't worth the fight. But you are.

This world profits from your self-doubt. It thrives when you second-guess yourself. It wants you to hate your body, question your worth, silence your emotions, and fit neatly into a mold that was never designed for you in the first place. Choosing to love yourself in a world that benefits from your insecurity? That's rebellion. That's resistance. That's war.

And reclaiming yourself, your voice, your strength, your identity after pain has tried to erase you? That's the fight of your life.

So, if you're ready to stop running from the things that haunt you...

If you're ready to sit with your pain instead of avoiding it...

If you're ready to face yourself, unfiltered and unedited, and do the work to heal...

If you're ready to give yourself permission to heal...

Then, welcome to The Struggle Show.

12

CHAPTER 12: GRIEF – THE HOLE THAT NEVER FULLY HEALS

But how lucky are we that we get to experience it?

I know that sounds wild. But think about it. Grief proves that we love so deeply and fiercely that even after someone is gone, love refuses to leave with them. It lingers, stretching across time and space, an unbreakable connection that even death can't sever. If that's not wild, I don't know what is.

Grief isn't a neat little five-step process. It's not an orderly progression where you cry, get angry, bargain with the universe, accept your fate, and then, poof, you're magically okay again. That's a fairy tale. That's the version of grief that people who have never actually experienced real, gut-wrenching loss like to believe in because it makes them feel better. The version allows them to put grief into a tidy little box, slap a bow on it, and pretend it's something they "get through" rather than something that becomes a permanent part of them.

But if you've ever lost someone, really lost someone, you know the truth.

Grief is chaos. It's an unpredictable, harsh, unforgiving shit storm that doesn't follow a timeline and doesn't care about how society thinks you should handle it. It's waking up and forgetting, just for a second, that they're gone, only to have reality punch you in the face all over again. It's feeling fine for one moment, and then, out of nowhere, a random song, a smell, or a stupid inside joke sucker-punches you so hard you have to stop and catch your breath physically. It's laughing at a memory one day and breaking down over the same memory the next. Knowing that no matter how much time passes, the world will always feel emptier without them.

It doesn't go away. Not in a week. Not in a month. Not in a year. Not ever. You don't "move on" from grief; you learn how to live with the hole it leaves behind. And yet, the world around you acts like you're supposed to "get over it" after some arbitrary period as if grief has an expiration date. It doesn't.

It can be ten years later and there will still be days when the loss feels fresh. You can rebuild your life, find joy, make new memories, and still have moments where the absence hits like a freight train out of nowhere. And that doesn't mean you're broken. That doesn't mean you're failing at grief. That just means you loved someone so damn much that their presence, and their absence, will always be a part of you.

And honestly? That's beautiful.

Grief is love that has nowhere to go. It's what happens when a connection so strong outlives the person it was tied to. It hurts because it matters. And while grief is a bitch, I wouldn't trade the pain if it meant never having had the love in the first place.

What Grief Feels Like

Grief is like getting hit by a tidal wave while standing in what you thought was knee-deep water. One second, you're okay, maybe even laughing, thinking you've got it under control. Then, out of nowhere, this massive, unforgiving wave slams into you, knocks you off your feet, and suddenly, you're underwater, gasping, panicking, unsure if you'll ever break the surface again. At first, it feels like you're drowning. Every time you try to stand up, another wave crashes over you. You're coughing up saltwater and wondering if this is how life is now. It's an endless cycle of getting your ass handed to you by something you can't even fight back against.

But over time, you start to learn the rhythm of the ocean. The waves don't stop, but you figure out how to brace for impact. You know when to dive under, when to ride it out, and when to float and let the current take you for a bit. You still get hit harder on some days than others, but you don't feel like you're drowning anymore. And eventually, you realize you've made it back to shore. Different than before, sure. You're saltier, maybe a little bruised. But you're still standing.

Grief is weird because it doesn't follow logic. It doesn't give you closure just because you want it. It doesn't show up in a way that's easy to explain. And most of the time, it makes you feel like you're losing your damn mind. It's not a clean-cut, predictable experience. It doesn't follow a timeline. It doesn't bow to expectations. It hits like a rogue wave, sometimes gentle enough to wade through, sometimes so powerful it knocks you under and leaves you gasping for air.

Grief is like waking up in a house, missing all the walls. You're still standing, but everything feels exposed and unsafe.

143

Like the structure that held your world together has been ripped away, you're just standing in the rubble, trying to figure out how to keep living when everything looks so different.

And here's what they don't tell you about grief:

It Makes You Forget Things

Ever been so deep in grief that you forget how to do your usual shit? Like eating? Sleeping? Responding to texts? Your brain short-circuits, and suddenly, existing feels like a task you're failing. You put your car keys in the fridge. You forget what day it is. You stand in the middle of a room without knowing why you walked in. Grief clogs up your mental bandwidth, leaving no room for basic functioning.

It Turns You Into A Walking Contradiction

One minute, you're numb. The next, you're crying over a commercial about a puppy. Five minutes later, you're laughing hysterically at something completely inappropriate. Then you're pissed off at the world for having the audacity to keep turning while yours has fallen apart. Grief doesn't make sense, and neither will you.

It Makes You Irrationally Angry

At people who don't deserve it. At yourself. At the sky. At the traffic light for taking too long. At the person you lost for leaving you, even if it wasn't their choice. At the world for continuing to spin like nothing happened. Grief turns you into a walking Molotov cocktail of emotions, and sometimes, you don't even realize you've lit the fuse until you explode.

It Sneaks Up On You

You think you're doing fine, and then, BAM, a random Tuesday knocks the wind out of you because you hear their favorite song in a grocery store. Or you find an old text they sent you. Or you call them before remembering that they'll never pick up again.

It Doesn't "Get Better," It Just Gets Different

You don't wake up one day and suddenly feel "healed." What happens is that, over time, you learn how to carry it better. It doesn't get lighter; you get stronger. Grief is like carrying a backpack full of bricks. At first, it's crushing. Every step is unbearable. The weight is too much. How am I supposed to live the rest of my life like this?

But then, slowly, without even realizing it, you adjust. You build muscle. You learn to shift the weight so it doesn't hurt as much. You still feel it, but it no longer stops you from moving. And one day, you look up and realize... you're carrying it without thinking about it every second of every day.

The weight never entirely disappears. But you grow strong enough to keep walking.

Grief Makes People Uncomfortable, So They Rush You

Society is terrible at dealing with grief. Like, genuinely fucking terrible. We live in a world that thrives on productivity, quick fixes, and pretending everything is okay even when it's not. And grief? Grief is inconvenient. Grief makes people uncomfortable. So, instead of supporting those who are grieving, society slaps a timeline on it and tells you to "move on."

Ever notice how, after someone dies, there is a short grace period during which people check in, bring you food, and offer condolences? But then, a few weeks later, the support fades. The world expects you to return to "normal," but they don't realize your routine no longer exists.

Society has unspoken grief rules. Take a couple of days off, but don't take too long. (Because capitalism doesn't give a shit about your pain.) Talk about your loss at first, but don't "dwell" on it. (People get uncomfortable when you're still grieving after what they consider a reasonable amount of time.) Smile and say you're doing okay, even when you're drowning. (Because people don't want the truth; they want to feel like they "checked in.") Find closure and move on. (As if closure is something you can buy at Target.)

Grief doesn't run on a schedule, but the world expects you to. Let's get something straight: closure is a myth. You don't "move on" from losing someone you love. You move forward with them still in your heart, learning to exist in a world that suddenly feels emptier.

Sometimes, We Cause Harm While Trying To Help

Look, most people mean well when they try to comfort someone grieving, and we have all been guilty of saying something the other person has heard 1,356 times. But let's be honest; some things we say resonate as harmful even though our intentions are pure. "Everything happens for a reason." Oh, does it? Please, tell me the reason my loved one is dead. I'd love to hear it. "They're in a better place now." That's cool, but I wanted them here. "At least they're not suffering anymore." Awesome, but I am. "You have to stay strong." Or what? I spontaneously combust? "They wouldn't want you to be sad." They also wouldn't want me to pretend I'm fine when I'm not!

Do you know what helps? "I'm here for you." (And actually, be there.) "You don't have to talk if you don't want to, but I'm here when you do." "I don't know what to say, but I love you." "Take your time. There's no deadline on grief." Grief isn't a problem to be solved. It's a reality to be witnessed. And the best thing you can do for someone who's grieving is to let them be in it without trying to fix it.

Sometimes, it's just sitting in the dark with someone bleeding for a bit of light. Some call it the Ministry of Presence; I call it **showing the hell up when words aren't enough.**

It's not about fixing, advising, or filling the silence with clichés that make *you* feel better. It's about sitting in the wreckage with someone and not flinching. It's about standing in the storm with them instead of waiting for it to pass. It's about resisting the urge to slap a Band-Aid on a bullet wound so that you can say you *did something.* Because sometimes, the most powerful thing you can do is just **be there.** No solutions. No platitudes. Just presence.

Learning To Live With Loss Without Losing Yourself

When you lose someone, the world doesn't stop. But you do. Everything around you looks the same, but nothing feels the same. The people around you keep moving, laughing, and going about their day like nothing changed while you're standing there, stuck in a reality you never asked for, trying to understand how the universe dared to keep spinning without them. It's like some cruel joke. One moment, they were here. The next, they weren't. And somehow, you're expected to figure out how to exist in a world without them.

So, how do you keep going when it feels impossible?

Let yourself grieve however, that looks to you.

There's no "right" way to do this. There is no manual, no step-by-step guide, and no perfect formula that makes the pain manageable. Forget what people tell you about how you should grieve. Screw the idea that you have to "process" it in some neatly packaged way. If you need to cry, cry. If you need to scream, scream. If you need to, sit silently and stare at the wall for three hours. If you need to talk about them constantly, talk. If you can't talk about them yet, that's okay, too. Your grief is yours. However it shows up, and it's valid.

Find ways to carry them with you.

Moving forward doesn't mean leaving them behind. It doesn't mean "letting go" or pretending like they never existed. They did exist. And they still matter. Hold onto the things that remind you of them: their laugh, their advice, their weird little quirks, the inside jokes only the two of you understood. Keep their stories alive. Say their name. Wear their favorite hoodie. Make their favorite meal. Carry them with you in ways that feel right to you. This isn't about staying stuck in the past. It's about keeping a part of them with you as you move forward. Because they were here, and they still matter.

Accept that grief isn't linear.

People love to act like grief is something you get through. It's like a road trip with a clear destination and an estimated arrival time, but that's not how this works. There will be good days. There will be awful days. And then there will be completely random days that hit you out of nowhere, knocking the wind out of you when you least expect it. You might feel "okay" one day and like you're drowning the next. You might go weeks feeling functional and then break down over something minor, like a song on the radio, a scent in the air, or the way a stranger laughs just like they did. That doesn't mean you're back at square one. That doesn't mean you're failing at grief. It just means you loved them. And love doesn't disappear just because someone is gone.

Don't let anyone rush you.

There is no expiration date on grief. There's no "should be over it by now." No universal timeline determines when you're supposed to feel okay again.

Some people will try to tell you otherwise. "It's been months." "It's been years." "Aren't you over this yet?"

Ignore them.

Grief takes as long as it takes. And the truth is, you don't get over losing someone you love. You learn to live with it. You learn to carry it differently. But there is no point where you magically wake up and say, "Okay, I'm done missing them now." That's not how love—or loss—works.

Take whatever time you need.

PERMIT YOURSELF TO HEAL.

This is the hardest part. The part that no one prepares you for. One day, you'll laugh again. You'll feel happiness creeping back in. You'll have a moment where you're genuinely okay, even for a little while. And then, just as quickly, guilt will sneak in. Like you're betraying them by moving forward. Like your joy is proof you've forgotten them. For example, if you keep living, you're leaving them behind. But you're not.

Grief isn't proof of love. Living is. Honoring them isn't about staying stuck in sadness forever; it's about carrying them with you as you step into whatever comes next. It's about making the most of the life they don't get to live anymore. You don't have to choose between holding onto them and moving forward. You can do both.

And the best way to honor the people you've lost? It is to live.

The Hole Never Fully Heals—And That's Okay

The Truth About Grief? It Never Really Ends. The hole never fully closes. The pain doesn't vanish just because time moves forward. You don't wake up one day "over it." That's not how this works. And that's okay. Because grief? Grief is love with nowhere to go. It's love that still exists, even when the person you gave it to is gone. It's every memory, every moment, every inside joke, every habit you picked up from them. It's how they shaped you and how their existence still lingers in your soul, even when the world expects you to "move on." But, they are not just from the past.

They are in everything that reminds you of them. They are in the way certain songs make you pause. On the way, a particular smell stops you mid-step. In the things they taught you, you now pass on without even thinking. They are in your laugh when you tell their favorite story. You still hear their voice when trying to make a tough decision. In the moments when you catch yourself doing something and think, damn, they would have loved this.

Grief doesn't mean you're broken. It means you shared. It means you explored. It means you took a chance. It means that you grew. It means that you achieved the most remarkable feat a human can. You loved. And if you're still feeling it, whether it's been months, years, or a lifetime, that love is still there. Always.

Because here's the truth: Grief is like an empty chair at your table. It doesn't matter how many years go by, how full the table gets, how much laughter and life continue around it; you will always notice the space. But that doesn't mean you stop eating. It doesn't mean you stop filling the room with joy. It just means you carry their absence with you, alongside everything else that makes life worth living. So, no, the hole may never fully heal. But that doesn't mean you can't build a life around it. That doesn't mean you can't find joy, peace, and happiness again.

Because grief isn't about forgetting; it's about carrying love forward in a new way.

13

CHAPTER 13: TRAUMA—THE WOUNDS YOU CAN'T ALWAYS SEE

Ah. My favorite topic. Why? Because it's something people think they can't heal from. It's something we believe will be waiting for us on our deathbed. The truth? It might be. If you don't address it. Trauma is a bitch. Not the dog kind. Not the what you call your mother-in-law kind. Trauma is the ultimate bitch. Not the petty, passive-aggressive coworker kind. Not the "stole your parking spot and smiled about it" kind. Trauma is the kind of bitch that breaks into your house, rearranges all your furniture, sets your bed on fire, and then gaslights you into thinking it was always that way. It's a home invasion of the soul, a hijacker of peace, a con artist that convinces you that safety is a lie and trust is a trap. Trauma is the kind of bitch that doesn't just hurt you, it rewires you. It makes happiness feel suspicious, love feel conditional, and rest feel criminal. It whispers doubts in your ear at 2 a.m., turns good memories into cautionary tales, and teaches you to flinch before life even raises its hand. Trauma is the kind of bitch that doesn't leave when asked. It lingers. It hides in the walls. It waits for quiet moments to remind you it still owns a piece of you. But, bitches can be evicted, and this is your notice to start packing its shit.

As a provider and recipient of Eye Movement Desensitization and Reprocessing (EMDR) therapy, I have a unique relationship with trauma. Here's what I've learned. Trauma changes you, rewires you, haunts you, isolates you, numbs you, shapes you, tests you, breaks you, rebuilds you, follows you, silences you, awakens you, scars you, confuses you, protects you, blinds you, hardens you, teaches you, exhausts you, steals you, consumes you, and tricks you.

Trauma isn't just for soldiers coming home from war or first responders who've seen some shit. It's not reserved for car crashes, violent assaults, or the kinds of massive, life-altering tragedies that make the news. If you've been walking around thinking, "Well, nothing that bad happened to me, so I guess I don't have trauma," stand by. Because trauma isn't just the big, dramatic moments that look like a movie scene, it's not always blood, sirens, and breaking news. Trauma can be quiet. It can be invisible. It can be the kind of pain that no one else sees, but it changes you. The kind that doesn't leave physical scars but rewires your entire brain.

The kind that doesn't come with medals, sympathy, or validation, just a quiet, constant reshaping of your nervous system, teaching you that the world isn't as safe, people aren't as trustworthy, and life isn't as predictable as you once thought.

Trauma is the parent who made you feel love was conditional like you had to earn it by being perfect, agreeable, or small. The friend who betrayed you in a way that still makes you second-guess trust. The time you were humiliated in public, and without realizing it, you started shrinking yourself to avoid being noticed. Your body tenses up when you hear a particular voice because, once upon a time, that voice meant danger. The relationship that made you doubt your reality left you questioning your instincts and wondering if you were the problem. The day you realized, for the first time, that the world isn't as safe as you thought it was.

Trauma isn't just the event itself; it's what happens inside you because of it. It's anything that overwhelms your ability to cope in the moment. And your brain? Your nervous system? They don't measure trauma by logic. They don't sit there weighing your experiences against someone else's to decide if you "deserve" to feel the way you do. Your brain doesn't care if someone else "had it worse." It doesn't care if no one else thinks it was a big deal. It doesn't care if you can't pinpoint the exact moment it happened. It only cares that something did happen. Something that made you feel unsafe, helpless, or out of control. Something that changes the way you move through the world, whether you realize it or not.

So, if you've been gaslighting yourself into thinking, "Maybe I'm just being dramatic. Maybe it wasn't that bad," let's clear this up right now:

If it changed you...

If it still lingers...

If it still affects how you see yourself, others, or life itself...

It was that bad.

And no, you're not crazy. You're not weak. You're not broken.

You're a human that went through some inhuman shit expecting a superhuman recovery.

Unrealistic expectations don't heal trauma.

Looking it in the fucking eyes does.

How Society Gaslights You Into Thinking "It Wasn't That Bad"

We live in a world that loves to minimize pain, especially if it's not visible. If you break your leg, people rush to sign your cast. But if you walk around with an invisible wound in your mind, people tell you to "get over it." And this is where the gaslighting begins. You open up about your trauma, and suddenly, the world starts handing you a list of reasons why you should shut the hell up about it: "Other people have been through worse." (So what? Does that mean I should be fine? Do we rank trauma now?) "You turned out okay, didn't you?" (Oh, sure. That's why I have trust issues, anxiety, and an occasional existential crisis.) "That happened a long time ago. Why are you still talking about it?" (Because my nervous system didn't get the memo to move on.) "But they didn't mean to hurt you." (My brain doesn't care about their intent—it remembers the impact.)

This is why people struggle to acknowledge their trauma. Because the second you start unpacking it, someone, somewhere, will try and stuff it back in the box for you. You don't need permission to name your pain. You don't need a dramatic, textbook definition of trauma to justify why something messed you up. You don't need anyone else's validation to start healing.

If it changed you, it matters.

156

The Four Trauma Responses: Fight, Flight, Freeze, Fawn

Ever react to something and think, "Why did I do that?" Maybe you shut down in a conflict when you should have spoken up. Maybe you lashed out when you should have stayed calm. Maybe you people-pleased your way through a toxic relationship without even realizing it. That's trauma. More specifically, that's your nervous system going into survival mode.

Fight: The Burn-It-All-Down Response

Fight mode isn't just throwing punches—it's any response where your brain decides, enough of this, we're going to war. It looks like Explosive anger or aggression. Constantly needing to "win" arguments. Feeling like you always have to be in control. Seeing everything as a potential threat to defend against and pushing people away before they can hurt you. For some people, fight mode works. Until it doesn't. Because living in a constant state of mental war is exhausting.

Flight: The "Run Before It Hurts You" Response

Flight mode is when your brain says, we're not dealing with this. Run. It shows up as Avoiding confrontation at all costs and constantly moving, achieving, or distracting yourself. Running from relationships when they get too close. Feeling restless, like you can never just "be." Using work, hobbies, or even travel as an escape. At first, flight mode seems productive. You get shit done. You're always on the move. But eventually,

157

you realize you're not running toward something—you're running away.

Freeze: The "I Don't Know What To Do, So I'll Do Nothing" Response

Freeze mode happens when your brain short-circuits. Instead of fighting or running, it just... stops. This looks like Shutting down during stress, dissociating (feeling numb or disconnected from reality), overthinking so much that you never actually act, feeling like life is happening to you instead of living it, and struggling to make small decisions. People in freeze mode get called lazy or unmotivated, but their brains are stuck in overwhelm mode. They aren't lazy; they're paralyzed.

Fawn: The "If I Make Everyone Happy, I'll Be Safe" Response

Fawn mode is when your survival strategy is to please the threat. This looks like Being a people-pleaser to the point of self-sacrifice. Saying "yes" when you mean "no." Avoiding conflict by smoothing things over, even when you're hurt. Feeling like your worth depends on how much you do for others. They struggle to set boundaries because "What if they get mad?"

People in fawn mode were often raised in environments where their needs weren't safe, so they learned to make themselves small. They knew that being agreeable kept them alive.

Reclaiming Your Mind From The Ghosts Of Your Past

The Worst Part of Trauma? It doesn't Stay in the past. It follows you. It seeps into your thoughts, relationships, reactions, and body. It's not just a bad memory that sits quietly in the background; it's a rewiring—a complete system override that turns everyday life into a battlefield you never signed up for.

Trauma lives in you. It's in the way your heart races for no reason. The way your stomach knots up when something feels off—even when there's no apparent danger. It's in the way you flinch at sounds, words, or memories that shouldn't still have this much power over you, but somehow, they do. You can tell yourself, "It's over." You can try to move on. You can bury it. You can pretend you're fine. But trauma doesn't give a damn about logic.

It lingers. It hijacks your nervous system, turning everyday situations into threats, safe moments into danger, and your mind into something you don't always trust. It shows up in the middle of the night, in the middle of conversations, in the middle of moments that were supposed to feel safe. It doesn't care about time. It doesn't care that you have things to do. It doesn't care that you want to be expected.

Trauma is like an overprotective bodyguard that won't stand down. It keeps flashing red warning lights, screaming, "We're under attack!" even when you're just standing in a grocery store or trying to enjoy a quiet evening. Your brain doesn't understand that the war is over, so it keeps reacting like the enemy is still around the corner.

But here's the good news: You don't have to let it own you. Healing from trauma isn't about erasing the past because that's not possible. It's about breaking the grip it has on your present. It's about loosening its fingers from around your throat, one moment at a time. It's about recognizing that you are not broken; your brain has been doing its job too well. It learned how to protect you at all costs, and now it needs to know that it's safe to put the weapons down.

It starts with reclaiming your mind.

Because trauma may have shaped you, but it doesn't have to define you unless you let it.

How To Start Taking Your Power Back

Name It

You can't fight a ghost you won't acknowledge. Call your trauma what it is. Stop minimizing it. Stop pretending it didn't affect you. Stop comparing it to someone else's pain like that makes yours invalid. If it changed you, if it still lingers, if it still controls how you move through the world—it counts.

Pay Attention To Your Triggers

What sets you off? What makes your heart race, stomach drop, and body tense? Your triggers aren't random; they're your trauma speaking. They're the breadcrumbs your nervous system leaves behind, pointing to wounds that never fully healed. Instead of ignoring them or shaming yourself for reacting, start listening. Your body is trying to tell you something.

Learn Your Default Trauma Response

Are you a fighter, always ready for a battle, even when there isn't one? Are you a runner, avoiding conflict, people, or places that remind you of the past? Are you a freezer, shutting down, numbing out, dissociating when things get overwhelming? Are you a people-pleaser, bending backward to keep the peace because survival once depended on it?

Understanding how your body reacts to triggers isn't about blaming yourself; it's about learning how to undo the patterns that trauma wired into you. Because once you see it, you can change it.

Practice Self-Regulation

Trauma rewires your nervous system. It convinces you that you're still in danger, even when you're safe. Learning to self-regulate—through grounding techniques, deep breathing, movement, therapy, and journaling, teaches your brain that you're not there anymore. That the war is over. That you survived.

You can't just think your way out of trauma. You have to teach your body safety again.

Set Boundaries Like Your Life Depends On It

Because honestly, it does. Trauma makes you think you have no control, but boundaries remind you that you do. You can say no, walk away, and protect your peace, even if it makes others uncomfortable.

Seek Real Help

Therapy isn't just for "broken" people; it's for people who are ready to take their power back and those looking to keep their demons at bay. And I say this as someone who's not just in the mental health field, but someone who's been in the chair. Someone who believed they were unsavable. Yet here I am. I am spilling my deepest ideas all over these pages for your enjoyment.

I know firsthand that trauma doesn't just "go away." Sometimes, no matter how hard you try, no matter how much you understand your trauma, it still lives in your body, waiting to be triggered. And for a long time, I thought I just had to live with that until I found EMDR (Eye Movement Desensitization and Reprocessing).

How EMDR Saved Me

As a law enforcement officer, I saw things most people don't even realize outside of movies. But one case, one moment in time, left a scar I didn't know how to heal. It controlled my every move. A two-month-old homicide victim whose last breath consumed my thoughts.

No training or preparation can make something like that okay. There is no way to just shrug it off or compartmentalize it into the standard-issue mental filing cabinet that cops are expected to use for trauma.

I carried that case with me for years. It followed me into my sleep, work, and sense of safety. No matter how much I tried to lock it away, it stayed.

Then, I found EMDR.

It didn't erase the memory. It didn't make me forget. But it broke the grip that memory had on me. The overwhelming emotional charge, the suffocating weight of it, EMDR took something that used to feel impossible and made it something I could live with. Something I could acknowledge without reliving it.

That's the power of real trauma work. And now, as an EMDR provider, I see this same shift in the people I work with. Trauma that once felt like a life sentence? It doesn't have to be.

So, if you carry more than you can handle alone, get help. You don't have to do this by yourself. And if you've tried therapy before and it didn't work, try again. The right kind of therapy, whether it's EMDR, somatic work, or something else entirely, can change everything.

What the Hell is EMDR? Let's Talk Filing Cabinets and Brain Clutter

Your brain is like a filing cabinet; every experience you've ever had gets processed, sorted, and neatly filed in its proper place.

But trauma? Trauma is that one chaotic, emotionally explosive file that refuses to go where it belongs. Instead of getting stored away like a regular memory, it gets stuck. It just sits out in the open, disorganized and raw. Every time you even brush past it, the drawer flies open, spilling everything over your mind like a disorganized stack of papers.

EMDR (Eye Movement Desensitization and Reprocessing) is like a highly skilled file organizer for your brain. Instead of forcing you to relive your trauma over and over again, EMDR helps your brain take that stuck file, process it properly, and finally put it in the right drawer.

The memory doesn't disappear, but it stops jumping at you every time you open the filing cabinet. It becomes just another document in the system instead of something that hijacks your entire day.

Another Way to Think About EMDR—The Broken Record Analogy

Imagine you're listening to a record (yes, we're going old-school with this one). But instead of playing smoothly, it's stuck on a scratch. It keeps repeating the same painful note. Over. And over. And over again. No matter how much you try to ignore it, your brain keeps replaying the trauma, the sights, the sounds, and the emotions on a loop. EMDR is like gently lifting the needle, smoothing out the scratch, and letting the song play through to the end. You don't forget the song. But it stops skipping. It stops keeping you locked in the exact painful moment. It lets you move forward, finally hearing the rest of the music. EMDR doesn't erase what happened. It changes how your brain holds onto it.

So, if you feel like you're drowning in old memories, if your past is still bleeding into your present, if you're exhausted from carrying things that refuse to stay buried, know that you don't have to keep living like this. You can get unstuck. You can move forward.

And EMDR might be the thing that finally lifts the weight off your chest. If it's not? Find what does. You're worth it.

Trauma Isn't Your Fault, But Healing Is Your Responsibility

You didn't ask for what happened to you. You didn't deserve it. And it most likely wasn't your fault. Even if it was, now you can decide how much power it still has over you. Healing doesn't mean forgetting. It doesn't mean pretending it never happened. It means standing in front of your trauma and saying, "You don't own me anymore."

Your past may have shaped you, but it doesn't have to define you.

It's time to S.H.I.F.T.

14

CHAPTER 14: MENTAL HEALTH: THE MIND IS A BATTLEFIELD

Mental health is the topic that society loves to pretend to care about until it's in their face. Until it's a friend, loved one, or even us. Then, all of a sudden, it becomes the last thing we want to talk about. Companies throw up a token post for Mental Health Awareness Month every year. Celebrities share their "It's okay not to be okay" tweets. Schools and workplaces toss around self-care and mental wellness as trendy buzzwords. But when it matters? When it's ugly? When it's real? When it's inconvenient? When it's personal? That's when the conversation suddenly gets quiet.

Because, let's be honest, most people aren't actually against mental health awareness. They don't want to deal with the reality of what mental illness looks like. We live in a world where physical health struggles are met with empathy, but mental health struggles? Those get met with judgment, skepticism, or straight-up dismissal. Break your arm? People rush to sign your cast. Break your mind? People start backing away like your struggles are contagious.

That's the double standard. People are comfortable with illness when they can see it, when it's tangible. When it makes sense to them, when it fits into their idea of what "struggling" should look like. But depression? Anxiety? PTSD? Bipolar disorder? Trauma responses? Those make people uncomfortable. Those force people to confront the fact that suffering isn't always obvious. That pain doesn't always come with a visible wound. Sometimes, the happiest-looking people are fighting battles no one else can see.

That doesn't fit neatly into an Instagram post.

The Mental Health Support That's All Talk, No Action

We live in a world that preaches "mental health matters" until it interrupts something. Call out of work because of the flu? "Get some rest! Feel better soon!" Call out of work because your depression is so bad you can't get out of bed? "Can you try to push through?" Cancel plans because you have a migraine? "No worries! Understandable!" Cancel plans because your anxiety is through the roof? "Come on, don't be dramatic."

Mental health awareness is all good until someone's symptoms inconvenience other people. Until someone's panic attack makes a room uncomfortable. Until someone's PTSD reaction doesn't look like the Hollywood version they expected. Until real human problems get spilled all over the dinner table, the conference room, and the cubicle, we all wear our little bracelets and share catchy trauma quotes.

Allow me to share a few of my experiences.

I have stood in the wreckage of gore and twisted metal left behind from a plane crash on my first day on the job as a state trooper. That didn't bother me. Standing in the wreckage of the family did.

Watching an infant take her last breath, knowing I could do nothing.

I stood between hate and hate during the Charlottesville riots.

Responded to the scene where a car had crashed into dozens of people, killing one, at the same event.

I handed a teenager his driver's license and gathered what was left of him off a tree 24 hours later.

I gave a man a courtesy ride who later committed murder.

I have told dozens of people that the most essential thing in their lives, the people they love the most, are not coming home.

I have held parents who have lost their children to suicide.

I have held children who have lost their parents to suicide.

I have stood in rooms, on scenes, and in auditoriums with THOUSANDS of first responders and family members who have lost and buried friends, family, and heroes.

I have held people together.

I have seen people torn apart.

I am 0-4 on CPR.

I have had a gun stuck in my face.

I have saluted friends who died at the hands of an evil world.

I have mourned friends who have died by their own hands.

I have been on a call in the middle of the night with someone holding the phone to one ear and a gun to the other, begging me for answers I didn't have.

Have you ever seen a person snap at the knees or waist and fall to the floor because the weight of their mental pain has finally caused their body to collapse? Or even if they just received bad news? I have seen it probably over a hundred times. One of those times? It was me at the mailbox in broad daylight after locating a St. Jude's card, which triggered a significant trauma. I hadn't met EMDR yet.

Here's what I've learned.

We all move through this world at our own pace, navigating as only we know how, completely oblivious to how everyone else is doing the same thing. We see everything the surface allows us to see.

We are oblivious to the wars behind the smiles of those we pass. We nod, wave, and continue. While they? They may be walking to the end of their line, and we'll never be the wiser.

So, we hide it. Avoid it. Pity it. Judge it. Minimize it. Dehumanize it. We bullshit it. No matter how heavy, we wear that mask because we can't tell the world the truth. Especially not the people walking by that we'll never see again.

And that's the problem. Society wants mental health struggles to be palatable, neat, clean, and quickly solved with a bubble bath, a motivational quote, or a quick pep talk.

But real mental health struggles?

They're sloppy. They're muddled. They don't always have a quick fix.

And if society cared as much as it claims to, it wouldn't just "raise awareness" during one month of the year. It wouldn't just tolerate mental illness when it's quiet, well-behaved, and easy to understand. It would show up for struggling people, even when it's inconvenient. It would listen without trying to slap a solution on something they don't understand. It would stop shaming people for the things they can't control because talking about mental health only matters if the support is confirmed. Otherwise, it's just another pretty post for social media.

The Reality No One Talks About

Mental health struggles aren't aesthetic. They don't come with soft lighting, cozy blankets, and a perfectly curated self-care routine. They're not just bad days that can be fixed with a bubble bath and an overpriced cup of herbal tea.

Genuine mental health struggles look like waking up exhausted no matter how much you sleep. Because your mind never indeed rests. Talking yourself out of every social interaction because the idea of pretending to be "fine" is exhausting. Feeling like you're drowning, even when everything in your life looks "okay" from the outside. Knowing you should reach out for help but convincing yourself no one cares. Struggling to find a reason to get out of bed, not because you're lazy, but because existing feels like too much some days. And the second you bring this up? The second you try to be honest about what's happening in your head? People start looking uncomfortable.

Because the world only wants to talk about mental health when it's digestible. They want the idea of helping people as long as it doesn't inconvenience them. They want to say, "You can talk to me!" but then get annoyed when you do.

They want to raise awareness in ways that don't make them feel responsible.

Because if they admit that mental illness is authentic, that it doesn't just go away with positive thinking, that people are suffering? Then they might have to do something about it. And most people don't want that responsibility. So, instead, they push it away. They change the subject. They make you feel dramatic or weak for struggling.

And that? That's why people don't talk about it. That's why

we say, "I'm fine," until our lungs give out while our brain screams for a life jacket. The world has made it very clear that your mental health struggles are only acceptable if they're wrapped in a pretty little bow. If they're palatable. Stubbed your toe? I've got time for that. Lost a loved one? I didn't know this conversation would require commitment, and now I want to leave.

Society has taught us that if our mental health struggles are real?

We'd better keep that shit to ourselves.

Why the "Just Be Happy" Advice is Useless and Insulting

Do you ever notice how people give the worst advice when you're struggling? "Just be happy!"

Oh, wow. Let me press the happy button real quick. Thanks, Karen. "Have you tried being grateful?" Right, because gratitude magically cures depression. Totally how that works. "Other people have it worse." Cool. And? Does that mean I should just shut up and suffer in silence? If someone is drowning, do you tell them to stop struggling because someone else is drowning deeper?

Look, people who say this shit aren't trying to be assholes (most of the time). They just don't get it. They assume mental health struggles are a choice. They think depression is just being "sad" and anxiety is just "worrying too much." They believe you wouldn't feel this way if you just tried harder. They don't understand that your brain is a wild ass cocktail of chemicals and hormones that sometimes doesn't mix perfectly. But they have no idea how to approach it because they can't see it.

Imagine your mind is like a house. It's warm, inviting, and maybe a little messy sometimes when in good shape, but it's still a place you feel safe in.

Depression isn't sadness. It's numbness. It's like watching your life happen from behind a foggy glass. It's knowing you should care about things but not being able to force yourself to. Depression is like someone coming in and painting all the windows with black paint. You know there's a world outside but can't see it. You can't feel the sunlight, even though you know it's there. You sit inside, staring at the walls, not caring enough to open the door.

Anxiety isn't just worrying. It's your brain treating every minor inconvenience like a life-or-death situation. It's overthinking every text, every conversation, every silence. It's living in a constant state of "something bad is about to happen," even when there's no actual danger. It's like having a smoke alarm that goes off whenever you toast bread. You can't tell the difference between a real fire and a burnt bagel, so you live on edge, bracing for disaster over things that shouldn't even be a threat.

Trauma doesn't just "go away" with time. It rewires your brain. It changes how you react to stress, process emotions, and trust (or don't trust) people. It stays with you, even when you think you've "moved on." It's like faulty wiring in the walls. You don't always see it, but it changes the house's functions. Maybe a light flickers, perhaps an outlet sparks, small reminders that something isn't right. And no matter how often you paint the walls or rearrange the furniture, the wiring is still deep in the foundation.

Telling someone to "just be happy" is like telling someone

with a broken leg to "just walk it off." You wouldn't say that because you understand that a broken bone needs treatment, support, and healing time. It's like walking into that house, seeing the blacked-out windows, the blaring alarms, the sparking wires, and saying, "Have you tried opening the curtains? Just turn the alarm off. Just rewire the house yourself."

Mental health isn't about "just trying harder." It's about fixing what's broken, piece by piece, with patience, support, and accurate help.

Depression, Anxiety, and the Daily Fight to Keep Your Head Above Water

People love to talk about depression and anxiety-like they're trendy little personality quirks like they're just cute, relatable struggles that make you "deep" or "mysterious." It's like posting "lol, my anxiety is so bad" memes on Twitter or romanticizing sadness in moody Instagram captions somehow captures what it's really like. But if you've lived with them, you know the truth. Depression isn't just feeling sad. It's feeling nothing. It's the heaviness in your chest that won't go away. It's like you're stuck in a body you don't recognize. It's losing interest in everything that once made you feel alive. It's watching people move through life effortlessly while dragging themselves through every day like they're wading through cement. And the worst part? You don't even know why. There's no apparent reason. There is no single moment you can point to. Just an endless fog that keeps pressing down, suffocating the parts of you that used to feel human. And anxiety?

Anxiety isn't just being stressed. It's a constant, unrelenting voice in your head whispering that something is wrong, even when everything is fine. It feels like the walls are closing in for no reason. It's replaying conversations repeatedly in your head, analyzing every word, wondering if you sounded weird or said something wrong. It's preparing for worst-case scenarios that will probably never happen, but your brain convinces you they will. It's apologizing for things that don't even require an apology because you can't shake the feeling that you're somehow too much and not enough at the same time. It's sitting in a room full of people and still feeling like you don't belong.

And then there's the exhaustion. Because anxiety and depression don't just live in your head; they drain you. Every decision feels overwhelming. Even basic things like responding to a text, getting out of bed, or making yourself a meal can feel impossible.

The Worst Part? You Get Good at Pretending You're Fine

Smiling when you're breaking inside. Going to work, showing up for people, keeping everything together while your brain is on fire. Cracking jokes so people don't realize how close you are to falling apart. Saying, "I'm just tired," because it's easier than explaining what's going on. Because society rewards the ones who suffer silently. Because nobody wants to deal with someone who's struggling visibly. Because the second you stop pretending? People start looking at you differently. They start acting awkward. They start pulling away. Because now it's not just a "relatable struggle." It's real, and most people

174

don't know how to handle it.

And that's why so many people fight these battles alone.

The Mask Gets Heavy.

At first, wearing the mask is a choice. You tell yourself, "I don't want to burden anyone. I can handle this." You convince yourself that it's just easier this way. But over time, the mask stops being something you put on; it starts becoming part of you. You wear it so well that even you start forgetting what's underneath. You become the one everyone can count on, even when you can't count on yourself. You master the art of keeping it together, even when you're seconds away from unraveling. And the longer you wear it, the heavier it gets.

It's like carrying a backpack full of bricks, but you can't take it off because everyone sees how much weight you've been carrying the second you do. That's terrifying. Because what if they don't know what to do with the real you? What if they see the exhaustion, struggle, and cracks and walk away?

So, you keep pretending. You keep performing. You keep showing up for everyone else, even when falling apart inside. Hear this; you were never meant to carry all this alone. The mask? It's a survival tool, but it's not supposed to be permanent.

And the right people? They won't run when they see what's underneath.

The Importance of Therapy, Support, and Unlearning Shame

Contrary to what I believed for most of my life, therapy is not a weakness. Asking for help is not a weakness. Taking meds is not a weakness. Admitting you're struggling is not a weakness.

Do you know what is weak? Shaming people for getting the help they need. Acting like mental health isn't just as important as physical health. Telling people to "just deal with it" instead of encouraging them to heal.

We live in a world where people will brag about never going to therapy like it's some achievement. Struggling in silence is seen as a strength, but seeking help is seen as a failure. Where taking medication for depression is considered "a crutch," but taking medication for high blood pressure is just responsible health care. And it's all bullshit.

If you broke your arm, would you be embarrassed to see a doctor? Would you sit there in agony, refusing medical attention because "I should be able to fix this on my own"? No? Then why should you be embarrassed to get help for your mind?

Because guess what? The brain is an organ, too; it tells all other organs what to do. So, we might as well invest in its health.

Trauma isn't something you just "shake off." Depression isn't a lack of gratitude. Anxiety isn't about being dramatic. PTSD isn't just "dwelling on the past." These conditions impact real people in tangible ways that can be just as debilitating as a physical injury.

And yet, the stigma remains.

Unlearning Shame—Because You Deserve Better

If you grew up in a "tough it out" culture and believed that struggling in silence was stronger than reaching out for help, let's clarify that mindset isn't strength. It's survival. Survival mode is not meant to be permanent. Strength isn't suffering alone. Strength is admitting, "I can't do this by myself." Strength isn't ignoring the pain. Strength is facing it head-on and working through it. Healing is not about being "tough." Healing is about being free. Free from the shame that tells you asking for help makes you weak. Free from the outdated belief that therapy is only for "people who can't handle life." Free from the weight of carrying something alone that was never meant to be taken alone.

So, if you're struggling? Get help.

Not because you're broken. Not because you're failing.

But because you deserve to heal.

The Stigma That Keeps People Stuck

The stigma around mental health is one of the biggest reasons people don't reach out. People don't avoid therapy because they want to suffer. They don't stay silent because they enjoy struggling. They avoid it because they've been conditioned to believe that asking for help makes them less than. They think it makes them a burden. They think it means they're damaged. They believe they must fix themselves before being loved, supported, or even taken seriously.

And that is just the right amount of...bullshit. Your struggles don't make you unworthy. Your trauma doesn't make you beyond repair. Your pain isn't something you have to hide to

177

be "acceptable."

The world has long convinced people that struggling makes them less than.

It's time we all unlearn that shit.

The Lies That Keep People From Getting Help

We live in a society that says "Mental health matters" but then turns around and shames people for actually struggling. If you ask for help, you're "weak." If you go to therapy, you're "crazy." If you take medication, you're "not trying hard enough." If you struggle openly, you're "seeking attention."

Meanwhile, if you bottle it up and suffer in silence? That's somehow seen as a strength. No wonder people stay stuck. No wonder people pretend they're okay while falling apart. Because when society only respects survival, not healing, people are forced to suffer quietly just to be accepted.

But we're "mental health aware."

No, we're not. But we damn sure want people to think we are.

Breaking the Cycle

Mental health isn't a luxury. It's not a trend. It's not something you can just "tough out." It's an exclusive club you didn't sign up for, but you keep paying the membership fees. You can't self-care your way out of trauma. You can't meditate your way out of PTSD. You can't "positive vibes" your way out of depression. Real healing takes work. And sometimes? It takes therapy, support, and medication. Not because you're weak. Not because you're broken. But because you deserve to get better.

So, if you've been putting off getting help because of shame, fear, or stigma, let me remind you of something:

Healing is your birthright. Not a privilege. Not a luxury. A right.

And anyone who makes you feel less than for wanting to heal?

They're the ones who need to unlearn some shit. Not you.

The Truth About Therapy & Healing

Write this down. Everyone has something going on. EVERY-ONE. Whether it's mild anxiety that makes social interactions feel like a chore, depression that turns getting out of bed into an Olympic event, or trauma that lingers in the background like a bad song stuck on repeat.

Some people are fighting battles so loud they echo grief, addiction, loss, and heartbreak. Others carry silent wars, which no one sees but still leave scars. The truth is no one makes it through life completely untouched. We all have something weighing us down, something clawing at the edges of our minds, something making us question if we're okay.

So maybe, just maybe, we stop assuming that everyone is okay just because they smile. Perhaps we should stop judging people for how they cope. Maybe we should take a second to ask, "Are you good?" And mean it. Because sometimes, the slightest acknowledgment of someone's struggle is the only thing keeping them from drowning.

Therapy is for everyone. You don't have to be in crisis to benefit from it. You don't need a "valid reason" to go. You don't need a diagnosis, a rock-bottom moment, or a life that's falling apart. If you have a mind, therapy can help. Period. Struggling in silence doesn't make you stronger. It just makes you lonelier. If you were never meant to heal alone, why should you suffer alone? You don't have to carry all of this by yourself. Some people love you, even when you feel unlovable.

You are not your mental illness. You are not your worst days. You are not the intrusive thoughts, the panic attacks, or the trauma responses that hijack your brain. You are a person. A whole, valuable, worthy person. And if you've ever thought to yourself, "I don't deserve help" or "I don't want to be a burden," listen to me right now.

You are not a burden. Your pain is not an inconvenience. You deserve to heal.

Period.

So Why Therapy? Why Now?

Not everyone needs intensive psychotherapy. Some need check-ins. Do you purchase a car and drive it until it dies? No oil changes? Tire rotations? Engine checks? Fluid refills? If you want your vehicle to perform, you must maintain it to last. Your house works the same way. Your relationships work the same way. Your company works the same way. Your body works the same way. Your MIND works the same way. Why maintain it?

Because you deserve better than just surviving. Because you deserve to feel at home in your mind. Because healing is not a privilege, it's a right. Therapy isn't just about "fixing problems." It's about learning how to live better. It's about unlearning the shit that's been weighing you down for years. It's about breaking cycles that have convinced you to settle for suffering.

Maybe you were taught to push everything down, be the "strong one," and "deal with it" alone. But where has that gotten you? Are you okay? Or have you just gotten good at pretending to be okay?

Because that's what this is, a fight. A fight for yourself. A fight for your future. A battle against a world that wants you to suffer in silence.

And the most challenging part? The enemy isn't just the world; it's the voice in your head telling you to give up.

15

CHAPTER 15: PURPOSE – FINDING MEANING WHEN LIFE FEELS POINTLESS

Ah. Purpose. The life-explaining ghost we're all chasing.

Have you ever noticed how every self-help book, TED Talk, and motivational speaker acts like purpose is some magical treasure buried deep in your soul, just waiting for you to find it? If you meditate hard enough, go on enough nature walks, or journal your feelings with a candlelit latte, your life's purpose will suddenly appear like a divine prophecy. You'll finally unlock the secret to happiness and success.

Yeah. No.

Purpose isn't something you find. It's something you create.

But society loves selling us this fairy tale version of purpose, this idea that every person has one singular, perfect, destined mission in life, and once you figure it out, everything will suddenly make sense. And if you haven't figured it out yet? Well, congratulations. You're failing at life. At least, that's what they want you to think.

The Lie That's Keeping You Stuck

This is why so many people spiral. They think if they don't wake up every morning feeling driven and fulfilled, something must be wrong with them. They think if they haven't "discovered" their true calling, they're doomed to a mediocre, meaningless existence. They believe they are somehow wasting their life if they're not passionate about every second of their job, hobbies, or daily routine. And that, if you haven't caught on yet, is bullshit.

Because most people don't have one singular purpose, they have multiple. And they change over time. You are not a character in a video game, wandering around waiting to unlock some final "Big Answer" that sets your path in stone.

Life is not a scavenger hunt. There's no playbook, checklist, or mystical moment where everything suddenly falls into place forever. Instead, life is a constant evolution—a process—a chaotic-ass journey of trying things, failing at things, discovering what matters to you, and, most importantly, not losing your mind.

The Truth About Purpose

We've been fed a massive lie about purpose.

We've been told that it is some grand, singular, life-altering mission, something that, once discovered, will give our lives instant meaning and direction. But that's not how it works.

Purpose Isn't Always Grand

You don't need to start a billion-dollar company, cure cancer, or climb Mount Everest to have a meaningful life. Sometimes, purpose is showing up for the people you love. Sometimes, it's creating, teaching, building, healing, learning. Sometimes, it's just getting through the day and knowing you tried. And guess what? That's enough.

Purpose Isn't Fixed

What matters to you right now might not be what matters to you in ten years, and that's okay. We evolve. We grow. Our purpose should, too. You are not a failure if you change paths. You are not lost just because you don't want what you once did. You can wake up one day and say, this isn't me anymore.

Purpose Isn't Something You Wait For

Sitting around, hoping that inspiration strikes, is a waste of time. The people who seem like they've "found" their purpose? They didn't find it. They built it through action, curiosity, effort, and sometimes, sheer accident. It isn't some mystical thing that lands in your lap. It's something you create by exploring, by trying, by doing.

Purpose Doesn't Have To Be Big To Be Meaningful

Not everyone is going to be a world-changing activist, a best-selling author, or a genius entrepreneur. But that doesn't mean your life is any less valuable. How you impact the people around you, how you show up, and how you contribute matters.

Purpose Doesn't Have To Be Loud To Be Important

Sometimes purpose is the quiet work of loving, listening, and lifting others up. Sometimes purpose is breaking a generational cycle, even if no one applauds you. Sometimes, it is just getting out of bed and trying again. And if you're sitting there thinking, I do not know what my purpose is...

That's normal.

It doesn't mean your life is meaningless.

Because purpose isn't a destination, it's not a title. It's not a singular achievement. It's a process. A journey. A choice. The real question isn't "How do I find it?" It's "What am I willing to create?"

It's time to stop waiting for purpose and start building it.

How Social Media Sells You a Bullshit Version of Success

If you've ever scrolled through Instagram at 2 AM while contemplating your existence, you already know the deal. Social media has made everything look like a perfectly curated highlight reel, including purpose. You see people who are "living their dream," and it makes you feel like garbage. You see influencers who "quit their 9-5 to travel the world", and suddenly, your job feels like a prison. You see someone your age who's "made it big," and now you're convinced you're falling behind. But here's the part no one talks about: Most people are faking it.

They're not always happy. They're not always fulfilled. Half of them are exhausted, broke, or secretly miserable, but they'll never show you that part because it doesn't fit the aesthetic. Social media has turned meaning into a performance. It's made it look like you're wasting your life if you're not hustling your passion into a seven-figure empire. But the truth is, purpose doesn't have to be profitable. It doesn't have to be glamorous. And it sure as hell doesn't have to be Instagrammable. Maybe your purpose today is just getting through the day without falling apart. Maybe it's helping one person, not changing the entire world. Maybe it isn't some vast, grand thing; it's just doing what makes you feel alive, connected, or valuable.

And guess what? That's enough.

So, stop measuring your purpose by someone else's perfectly edited story. Because comparison is the fastest way to convince yourself that your life is meaningless, and that's not reality.

The Myth of a "Singular" Purpose

One of the most dangerous lies we've been fed is that we each have one true purpose in life, and if we don't find it, we've failed. This is why so many people get stuck. They think if they pick the "wrong" career, the "wrong" passion, or the "wrong" path, they're screwed. But that's not how life works. Again, most people have multiple purposes throughout their lives.

Think about it. What mattered ten years ago probably isn't the same thing that matters to you now. The things that made you feel fulfilled in your twenties won't necessarily fulfill you in your forties. Your passions, values, and priorities all shift as you grow. So, why do we act like we have to lock ourselves into one purpose and never change? Purpose is fluid. It evolves with you. And the second you stop treating it like some Holy Grail you have to "discover," you'll stop driving yourself crazy trying to find it.

I know this firsthand because I lived it.

For years, I thought law enforcement was my purpose. It wasn't just a job; it was who I was. The uniform, the badge, and the service all felt like what I was meant to do. And for a long time, it was. It gave me that sense of purpose. It gave me an identity. It made me feel like I was making a difference. I lived it. Breathed it. I couldn't stand being home because I'd rather be working.

But life has a funny way of shaking you out of certainty.

After years in the field and seeing things most people will never have to know, I started to feel a shift after feeling the weight of the job in ways I didn't even realize. The job was still important, but something in me was pulling in a different direction. I saw the toll it took on people, the silent struggles, the unspoken battles. I saw officers breaking under the weight of everything they carried, and I knew the system wasn't built to support them the way it should. I saw the shattered pieces of my brain and heart restored to something manageable after I was ready to give up.

That's when I realized my purpose wasn't just serving as an officer but also helping officers, first responders, and anyone else fighting silent battles. So, I walked away from the uniform full-time and entered the world of mental health.

That was a terrifying shift. Because when something has been your entire identity, letting it go feels like losing yourself. But I wasn't losing myself; I was evolving. I don't regret a second of my time in law enforcement. That was my purpose then. But I also don't regret walking away. Because this is what I do now, this is my purpose now.

Maybe my purpose will shift again. And that's okay. Because it isn't a singular, unchanging thing; it's a living, breathing part of you.

The biggest mistake is believing we must find one purpose and never stray from it. But if we permit ourselves to change, grow, and evolve, we stop fearing "getting it wrong" and start living the life we're meant to live.

Creating Meaning (Without Losing Your Mind Trying to "Find" It)

If purpose isn't some magical thing you "find," how do you create it?

Here's the key: Stop looking for it like it's a destination. Start creating it through action. Stop Overthinking and Do Something. Too many people waste their lives waiting to "find" their purpose instead of trying things to see what resonates. "I don't know what I'm passionate about." → Okay, try new things. You won't find your purpose by sitting around overthinking. "I don't know what I'm meant to do." → No one does until they start doing shit. You can't "think" your way into purpose—you must experiment. "What if I pick the wrong thing?" → Who cares? If it doesn't fulfill you, you can change course.

Start small. Try things. Explore. Follow curiosity, not pressure. Purpose isn't a pre-written script but an improv show.

Focus on What Matters to You

Not what your parents expect. Not what society says is "impressive." It's not what looks good on social media. What makes you feel alive? What makes you feel valuable? What would you do even if no one applauded you for it? What makes you forget to look at your phone?

That's where meaning starts.

Let Go of the Idea That Purpose Has to Be Huge

Some of the most meaningful lives aren't built on big, world-changing missions but on small, everyday actions that make a difference to someone. If you make one person feel seen today, that's purpose. If you create something that brings you joy, that's purpose. If you show up for the people you love, that's purpose.

You don't need to be the next Steve Jobs, Oprah, or Elon Musk to live a meaningful life.

You must be intentional with what you do, who you help, and how you show up.

Accept That Some Days, it Looks Like Survival

Not every day is going to feel meaningful. Some days, your only job is to make it to tomorrow—and that's okay. Stop chasing constant fulfillment. Stop expecting purpose to feel amazing every second. Some of the most important things you'll ever do will feel boring, exhausting, or downright pointless in the moment. But over time? Those small, consistent actions build a life that matters.

I see this firsthand in my nonprofit work with first responders. We had an out-of-state participant at a seminar who was in a terrible place, one of those moments where everything felt too heavy or impossible. After a long conversation, I told her, "Just make it one more day." Someone needs you, even if you can't see it right now. Later, she sent me a picture of the beach and the sand; she had written One More Day.

That moment stuck with me. I started sharing her picture in presentations, and in every class, someone approaches me about getting help. I've told her, you likely saved a life today. And never said a fucking word. Her energy. Her story. Her vulnerability. Her resilience. Her strength. It carried someone through the worst time of their life. Here's the crazy part.

The likelihood of them ever meeting is as close to zero as possible. That's the power of your healing. Your healing can save lives. I experience this weekly.

A year after the first picture, she sent me another. Different beach. Same message. One More Day.

She had found the love of her life, and she was thriving. And just by telling her story, she saved the lives of people she had never met.

Purpose isn't always about grand gestures or perfectly planned paths. Sometimes, it's as simple as holding on for one more day. It's not always big, glamorous, or obvious; it's often found in the slightest, quietest moments.

So, stop obsessing over whether you've "found" your purpose.

Instead, ask yourself: Am I doing things that matter to me? Am I showing up in a way that feels meaningful? Am I living in a way that I won't regret later?

If the answer is yes, even in small ways, then congratulations.

You're already living with purpose.

And if the answer is no?

Well, good news. You can change that shit right now.

I'm writing this book because I've realized something important. Finding my purpose wasn't about luck. It wasn't some cosmic lottery I happened to win. My purpose didn't just find me; it was forged in every experience, every hardship, every moment I thought I was breaking but was being built.

And the people who benefit from it? That's not luck, either. That's the ripple effect of turning pain into something bigger than myself. The purpose isn't about being chosen; it's about choosing. And I prefer this. I decide to take what I've learned and what I've lived and put it into words so that someone else, someone who feels lost, numb, or defeated, can see that their story isn't over. It's just shifting.

16

CHAPTER 16: PERSPECTIVE – HOW TO STOP SCREWING YOURSELF OVER

Perspective. It's the lens you see through, and it shapes everything.

How you see yourself, your past, your circumstances, the world, and the people around you is the foundation of your life. And if your perspective is warped, if you see things through a lens of self-doubt, victimhood, or unprocessed trauma, guess what? Your life is going to reflect that.

Now, before you roll your eyes and think I'm about to sell you some "just think positive" bullshit, hold up. This isn't some toxic positivity cult nonsense. This isn't about ignoring reality and pretending that life is all sunshine and unicorns. This is about authentic, raw, game-changing perspective shifts that help you stop making your life harder than needed.

Because let's be honest, most of the time, the most significant thing standing between you and the life you want... is you. Yes, the world is a mess. Yes, life is unfair. Yes, people suck sometimes. But at the end of the day? The way you react, the way you think, and the way you frame what happens to you will determine whether you spend your life feeling like a powerless victim or a force of nature.

The Power of Perspective: The Fork in the Road

Two people can go through the same situation, hell, the same trauma, and come out completely different. One will be bitter, broken, and convinced the world is out to get them. The other? They'll rise, get stronger, and turn that pain into fuel.

The only difference between them?

The lens through which they see life.

And here's the kicker: your lens wasn't entirely built by you. From the moment you were born, the world started handing you filters. Your family. How they saw themselves and the world shaped you before you even had a say in it—your culture. What you were taught about success, failure, relationships, and happiness shaped what you believed was possible—your experiences. The good ones taught you hope, but the bad ones? They left marks still shaping how you trust, love, and move through the world. Your pain. The things that hurt you changed how you see yourself, whether you realize it or not.

Some of these filters gave you strength. Others? They've blinded you, keeping you in a self-sabotage, doubt, or fear cycle. You weren't born insecure. You weren't born afraid to take risks. You weren't born believing you weren't good enough.

You learned that shit.

It's time to unlearn it.

You Don't Have to Keep Looking at Life Through a Cracked, Bullshit-Covered Lens

You get to clean that shit up. You get to change how you see things. You get to take control of your perspective, which will always be yours. Perspective isn't just some passive, feel-good mindset shift. It's a weapon. It's your most excellent tool for survival, growth, and transformation. Because when you learn to control how you see things, you learn to control how you respond to them. When you shift your perspective, you move your power.

And when you shift your power?

You shift your entire damn life.

Self-Sabotage: The Art of Screwing Yourself Over

Have you ever caught yourself doing something that you know is bad for you, but you do it anyway? Procrastinating on shit you care about? Sabotaging relationships that are good for you? Talking yourself out of opportunities? Convincing yourself you'll fail before you even try? I do all the damn time.

That's self-sabotage, baby. And it's one of the most common ways people jack up their own lives without even realizing it. The worst part? Most self-sabotage isn't loud and dramatic. It's quiet. Subtle. Sneaky as hell. The tiny, daily choices keep you stuck: The job you don't apply for because "I'm not qualified enough." The boundaries you don't set because "I don't want to upset them." The dreams you never chase because "What if I fail?" The toxic cycles you keep repeating because "That's just who I am."

Sound familiar? That's because self-sabotage is usually

driven by fear and limiting beliefs that got wired into your brain long ago. The solution? You have to start catching yourself in the act.

How to Break the Cycle of Self-Sabotage

Catch the Pattern

Notice when you repeat behaviors that don't serve you. Ask yourself, "Is this actually what I want, or is this just my fear talking?"

Challenge the Thought

When your brain tells you, "You can't do this," respond with, "Why the fuck not?" Seriously. Demand receipts from your brain.

Do It Anyway

The scariest part? Action. But guess what? You don't have to feel confident to take action. Sometimes, you have to do it scared.

Reframing Without Gaslighting Yourself

Wait. Can I gaslight myself?

You bet. And you probably do it all the time.

We've already established that perspective shapes reality. But let's discuss a mistake many people make when trying to "think positive" or "change their mindset."

It's called gaslighting yourself, aka pretending shit isn't happening, instead of dealing with it.

Toxic Positivity vs. Healthy Reframing

Toxic positivity gaslighting: "Everything happens for a reason! Just be grateful!" (Translation: Your feelings aren't valid. Stuff them down and smile.) Healthy perspective shift:

"This situation sucks, but I have the power to decide how I respond." (Translation: I can acknowledge my pain AND still choose to move forward.)

See the difference? One is bullshit denial. The other is empowerment.

You're Allowed to Feel What You Feel

You're allowed to admit when things are hard. You're allowed to be angry, hurt, or frustrated. You can say, "This isn't fair, and I hate it." Pretending everything is fine when it's not doesn't make you strong. It makes you disconnected from reality. And being disconnected from reality is a dangerous place to live. Why? Because you can't heal from or change what you pretend isn't a problem.

If you're constantly telling yourself, "It's fine, I'm fine, everything is fine," when it's very much NOT fine, you're not "being positive." You're gaslighting yourself into ignoring what needs to be dealt with. And the problem with forgetting things? They don't go away. Pain doesn't just disappear because you pretend it isn't there. It festers. It turns into resentment. It sneaks into your habits, your reactions, your relationships. It owns you from the shadows.

196

Reframing isn't about lying to yourself.

It's about honestly examining a situation, accepting the parts you can't change, and shifting your focus to what you can control.

Reframing Is NOT About Excusing Shit That Shouldn't Be Excused

This is important. Reframing is NOT: "Well, maybe they didn't mean to hurt me..." (when they did) "Maybe it wasn't that bad..." (when it was) "I should just be grateful it wasn't worse... " (as if the pain has a minimum threshold before it's valid)

No. Screw that. Sometimes, bad things happen for no good reason. Sometimes, people hurt you because they're selfish and cruel. Sometimes, life is straight-up unfair. And you know what? You're allowed to say that out loud.

You don't need to sugarcoat your past to make it easier to swallow.

What you do need is to decide what you're going to do with it.

Your Past Might Not Be Your Fault, But Your Healing Is Your Responsibility

Yeah, life has thrown some shit at you that you didn't deserve. Yeah, people have done things to you that weren't your fault. You still have to choose how you frame your story. You still have to decide what happens next. Do you let it define you? Do you let it own you? Or do you take that pain, that bullshit, and make something out of it?

Because, at the end of the day, that choice is where your

power is.

Your Brain is a Storyteller, Make Sure It's Telling the Right Story

Your brain? It's a novelist. It takes the things that happen to you and creates a narrative. But here's the catch: you get to decide whether you're writing a tragedy, a horror, or a redemption story. And let's be honest, most people are out here writing themselves into a lifetime of misery without even realizing it. Not because they want to, but because they've been telling the same negative story for so long that it feels like truth.

But truth and perspective? Two very different things.

You get rejected from a job you wanted.

Negative Story: "I'm a failure. I'll never be good enough. I shouldn't even try anymore."

Reframed Story: "That wasn't the right fit for me. Rejection isn't the end—it's a redirection."

You go through a breakup.

Negative Story: "I'm unlovable. I'll be alone forever."

Reframed Story: "This hurts like hell, but I'd rather be alone than in something that wasn't meant for me."

You feel stuck in life.

Negative Story: "It's too late for me. I'll never get where I want to be."

Reframed Story: "I might be stuck now, but every day is a chance to shift in a new direction."

This isn't about sugarcoating reality. It's not about pretending that pain doesn't exist. It's about recognizing that how you frame that pain determines what you do with it.

Because your brain isn't just telling a story. It's believing it.

If you keep feeding it narratives of failure, rejection, and hopelessness, guess what? That's what it will look for. Your brain is wired to confirm the beliefs you hold. So, if you believe you're destined to fail, your mind will highlight every moment that proves that belief right.

But the opposite is also true. If you tell yourself that setbacks are setups for something better, that rejection is redirection, and that struggle builds resilience, your brain will look for those patterns instead.

The stories you tell yourself shape your reality. And if you've been telling yourself a shitty story? You're reality will play out like a shitty story.

Change the narrative.

The Power of a Perspective Shift

A positive perspective doesn't mean ignoring real problems. It means you stop giving those problems more power than they deserve. Because when you zoom out, shift your lens, and look at the bigger picture? A lot of the shit you're stressing over isn't as permanent, consequential, or personal as it feels in the moment.

Recognize That Most Things Are Temporary

No matter how bad things feel, they won't last forever. Life is constantly changing, and that means your struggles will, too.

Separate Facts from Feelings

Feeling worthless doesn't equal being worthless.
Feeling stuck doesn't equal being stuck forever.
Feeling scared doesn't equal being incapable.
Your brain is loud, but it's not always right.

Find the Lesson (Without the Clichés)

Not every struggle is a "blessing in disguise." Some shit sucks. But that doesn't mean you can't learn, grow, and become stronger.

Focus on What You Can Control

You might not control everything that happens to you. But you can control how you respond. And sometimes, that's the difference between sinking and swimming. Your perspective is your power. And the way you frame your life determines whether you feel like a victim of circumstance or the main character in your own story.

So, here's your challenge: Start catching yourself in the act of self-sabotage. Start questioning the bullshit stories your brain tells you. Start shifting your mindset in a way that empowers you, not in a way that gaslights you. And most importantly, stop making your life harder than it needs to be.

The only person who can truly change your life... is you.

Control what you can. Adapt to the rest.

The most important lesson I've ever learned is that when something terrible or inconvenient happens to me, I tell myself, "If this is the worst thing that happens today, it's going to be a good day."

That spilled coffee won't kill me. That asshole in traffic is already gone. That argument I didn't win is already over.

I have seen bad days. I've witnessed hell. Hell, I've lived it. I've seen bad days.

And this ain't it.

III

PART III: WELCOME TO THE S.H.I.F.T. SHOW™

*Now that you see the world clearly and have faced the struggle, it's time to take control. This is where the fundamental transformation begins. Using the **S.H.I.F.T.** Framework™—Stop, Hype, Innovate, Fight, Thrive—you'll learn how to rewrite your story on your terms. No more waiting, no more excuses. It's time to step into your power, own your life, and create the future you deserve. The world won't change for you, but you can change how you move through it. Hell, maybe you'll change it.*

17

CHAPTER 17: WELCOME TO THE S.H.I.F.T. SHOW ™

Welcome to the moment you've been waiting for.

Or dreading.

It depends on how attached you are to the bullshit you've been carrying. Either way, Welcome to The S.H.I.F.T. Show.

This is where we stop discussing the chaos, the problems, the world's dumpster-fire tendencies, and your collection of demons. We've covered all that. We've dragged all the skeletons out of the closet, laid them on the table, and stared them in the face. Now? Now, we do something about it.

This is where we introduce the star of the show. The S.H.I.F.T. Framework™. It's where we stop being passive participants and take the wheel. And if you're already bracing for impact, thinking, shit, this is going to require effort, then good. You're getting it.

Because real change is not about reading a book, getting inspired, and then returning to your regularly scheduled programming; it's not about nodding along, highlighting a few quotes, and telling yourself, "Wow, this was deep," before shoving it back on the shelf next to all the other books you meant to apply to your life but didn't.

The S.H.I.F.T. Framework is where excuses go to die. It doesn't require perfection. It requires permission. You permitting yourself to change the shit that has been holding you back.

Imagine your life as a car. You've been riding in the passenger seat for years, maybe even your entire existence. Perhaps someone else has been driving. Maybe trauma took the wheel a long time ago. Possibly, society, expectations, or fear have gripped that steering wheel so tight that you forgot you even had a say. Well, guess what?

You do.

This? This is where you grab the wheel and take back control. It won't be smooth. It won't be easy. There's a reason most people stay in the backseat, complaining about the ride instead of taking control of where they're going.

Because change is work, it's uncomfortable. It's a mental brawl. And most people? They don't do it. They don't want to get awkward, not because they can't. They don't want to sit with the truth that they keep themselves stuck.

But you? You're still here. And that means something.

It means some part of you, maybe a small part, perhaps a loud, screaming part, knows that you're meant for more.

Knows that you've been sleepwalking through life, carrying baggage that was never yours to hold, following rules that don't serve you, and waiting for some external force to come along and fix everything.

But no one is coming to save you. Not society. Not your family. Not a relationship. Not some magical stroke of luck. If you want your life to change, you have one option: You have to change it yourself. And that's where S.H.I.F.T. comes in.

This isn't just some cute acronym. This isn't about empty motivation or half-assed life advice. This is about doing the work, the complex, hard, sometimes painful, but always worth it kind of work. Do you want better? Do you want more? Do you want a life that feels like yours instead of something you endure?

Then buckle up because this isn't just another chapter. This is the turning point. This is where the old version of you gets left behind, the one weighed down by fear, self-doubt, and all the stories you were told about who you should be. In its place? A version of you who knows their worth. A version of you who fights for themselves. A version of you who stops waiting and starts moving. It won't be easy. But nothing worth it ever is. And trust me, this? This is worth it because you are.

The Five-Part Blueprint for Changing Your Life: The S.H.I.F.T. Framework

We've covered the chaos. We've dissected the systems. We've called out the bullshit.

Most people don't change, not because they can't, but because they don't know where to start. They don't realize they're playing by rules never made for them. They don't see the trap until it's too late. That's why S.H.I.F.T. isn't just some catchy acronym. It's the blueprint. It's how you stop living at the mercy of everything and everyone else and start owning your damn life. This is not about making minor, comfortable tweaks.

This is about radical self-ownership.

The Five Steps to Breaking Free

S: Stop – Quit Giving Power To The Bullshit That Drags You Down

Your energy is limited, so why are you wasting it on things that drain, control, and diminish you? If something isn't helping you, growing you, or strengthening you, it's dead weight. Drop it. Stop obsessing over opinions that don't pay your bills. Stop fighting battles that aren't even yours. Stop looking for permission to take up space.

If you want real change, the first step is to clear the damn clutter.

H: Hype – Pump Yourself Up Like You Belong In Your Spotlight

If you don't believe in yourself, why should anyone else? If you walk through life like a supporting character in your own damn story, waiting for someone to validate you, crown you, or save you, guess what? You're going to be waiting forever. This is where you switch narratives. Talk to yourself the way you'd talk to someone you love. Find your wins, no matter how small, and celebrate them as they matter. Recognize that confidence isn't something you "have," it's something you build.

If you want to thrive, you must hype yourself up, as your life depends on it because it does.

I: Innovate – Reinvent Your Approach To Life

The world tells you to color inside the lines, but guess what? Those lines? They were drawn by people who don't even know you. Who told you success has to look a certain way? Who decided failure means the end of the road? Who made the rules you're still unthinkingly following? Most systems you've been following are outdated, broken, or built to keep you small. It's time to break them. Innovation isn't about burning your life down for the hell of it. It's about recognizing that if the old ways aren't working, you don't have to keep forcing yourself to fit into them.

F: Fight – Stand Your Ground Against The Chaos

Life is coming for you whether you like it or not. You will have bad days. You will have setbacks. You will have moments where you feel like giving up. But what is the difference between people who stay stuck and people who rise? They fight. Fight against the self-doubt that tells you you're not good enough. Fight against the conditioning that says you must be small, silent, or obedient. Fight against the urge to quit just because it's hard. You've been through worse. You've survived things that should have broken you.

You are stronger than the chaos.

T: Thrive – Live Unapologetically On Your Damn Terms

This is what it all builds up to—not just surviving. Not just existing. Not just cruising along but living. Thrive means taking up space without apologizing for it. Thrive means choosing joy, even when the world wants you to be miserable. Thrive means owning your life so thoroughly that no one else can dictate how you experience it. Most people live life like they're waiting for something.

Waiting for approval. Waiting for confidence. Waiting for the "right time."

Here's the truth:

There is no "right time."

The only time you can manipulate is right now. Here. The present moment.

We'll break down the S.H.I.F.T. Framework and its application in your life in more detail later, but first;

Is the Map You're Following Yours? Or Someone Else's?

You're either in the driver's seat of your life, or you're letting someone else steer. And if you're letting someone else steer? Newsflash: They don't give a shit if you crash. The world will happily dictate who you should be, what you want, and how you should live if you let it.

Society has built an entire system around keeping people passive, doubtful, and stuck. Why? Because people who don't believe in their power are easier to control. But you're not here to be controlled. You're not here to live on autopilot, waiting for someone to hand you permission to exist on your terms.

The S.H.I.F.T. Framework is about breaking free from that.

It's about reclaiming your mind, choices, and life.

This is the Moment You Decide

Are you going to keep letting the world write your story for you? Or are you going to grab the pen and rewrite the whole damn thing? Because this is the turning point. The moment you stop looking for answers outside of yourself and start realizing the power has been yours all along. This isn't just a framework. This is your blueprint for freedom.

The Cost of Staying the Same

Let me ask you something: what's the price of staying exactly where you are?

What's the cost of not changing? Of not facing your patterns, not setting boundaries, not breaking cycles, not walking away from what doesn't serve you, not standing up for yourself? Because there is a cost. Maybe it's your happiness. Perhaps it's your peace. Maybe it's your sanity. Maybe it's the version of you that you were meant to become but never will because you were too afraid to burn the old version down. And if that reality doesn't sit right with you? Good.

You're ready.

Because you don't have to stay stuck, you don't have to keep living by default. You don't have to wait for permission to be who you were always meant to be.

So, Welcome to the S.H.I.F.T. Show.

18

CHAPTER 18: HATE – THE POISON THAT'S RUINING EVERYTHING

Hate. I hate it. I hate hate. Hate is the poison that seeps into the cracks of humanity, turning connection into division. The toxin infects minds and is passed down like a sickness disguised as tradition. The venom paralyzes progress, keeping us locked in the same tired battles, generation after generation.

Hate is a fire that doesn't only burn its target; it scorches everything around it. It turns people into strangers, strangers into enemies, and the world into a battlefield where no one truly wins. And the worst part? Most people drinking the poison don't even realize they're the ones being destroyed by it.

Let's talk about hate. Not in a fake, watered-down, "we should all just love each other" way, but in an honest, unfiltered, let's-call-this-shit-out way. Because if we're being honest? Hate has become the most contagious disease in the world.

It's in our politics. It's in our social media feeds. It's in our communities, families, conversations, and thoughts. It's everywhere. And the worst part? Most people don't even realize they're infected. They justify it. They dress it up as "just having an opinion." They call it "standing up for what's right." They pretend it's about morality, justice, or protecting their way of life. But at the end of the day?

Hate is fear in a cheap disguise.

Hate is Engineered

Nobody is born hating. But damn, do they learn fast. Look around—entire industries profit from keeping people divided. Social media algorithms thrive on outrage. The angrier we are, the more we engage. The more we engage, the more they profit. Facebook, Twitter, TikTok, they don't care about "truth" or "unity." They care about clicks, shares, and ad revenue. And nothing spreads faster than rage. Politicians fuel their careers by stoking fear. The easiest way to stay in power? Convince people they're under attack. Make them believe that someone, the other party, another race, another country, or another belief system, is trying to destroy them. And when people feel threatened? They stop reasoning. They don't want solutions. They want a target. News outlets feed on conflict. "If it bleeds, it leads" isn't just a catchy saying; it's a business model. They know that calm, thoughtful discussions don't make people tune in. But a fight? A scandal? A controversy? That keeps people watching. That keeps them addicted. Hate is an economy. Think about it. How many industries thrive off division? Gun sales skyrocket when people fear the "other side." Security companies profit when people feel unsafe. Political donations surge when people believe their opponents are monsters.

We are being played. And we keep buying in.

We're Not Just Witnessing History

Hate isn't new. But every time it happens, people act shocked. Remember the Holocaust? It was a genocide fueled by fear, propaganda, and the belief that one group was "the problem." Millions of people were slaughtered, not by monsters, but by ordinary citizens who bought into the lie. Remember segregation? People once believed, with absolute certainty, that skin color determined worth. People of different races shouldn't share schools, water fountains, or even seats on a bus. And they justified it. Just like people today justify their brand of hate.

Let's not pretend we've evolved. We still have cages for kids at borders. We still have people who think someone else's existence threatens theirs. We still have governments banning books, silencing voices, and rewriting history to fit a more "comfortable" narrative. This is not new. And yet, every time hate boils over, people act surprised. Every time another hate crime happens, every time another war breaks out, every time another marginalized group gets targeted, people say, "I can't believe this is happening."

Really? You can't believe it?

We've seen this movie before. We've seen the prequel and the sequel. We know the outcome. But we keep watching the same damn movie on repeat, expecting a different result.

That's the literal definition of insanity.

Hate is an Addiction, And We're Hooked

Here's the brutal truth: Hate feels good. That felt weird coming off the lips, right? Or it sounded strange in whatever your reading voice sounds like. Wait. Is my reading voice just.......my voice? I have a master's degree.... And you thought I was smart.

Hate gives us a rush. It makes us feel righteous. It provides us with a target for our frustrations. And most importantly? It lets us avoid looking inward. Because it's so much easier to point fingers at "those people" than to confront our biases, fears, and insecurities. It's easier to believe that our enemies are the problem than it is to accept that maybe—just maybe— we've been conditioned to see the world in a way that keeps us angry and afraid. We pick our sides. We build our echo chambers. We convince ourselves that our brand of hate is justified. We tell ourselves it's different when we do it. "It's not hate, it's just the truth." "I don't have a problem with them; I just think they're ruining society." "I'm not racist/homophobic/sexist; I just believe in traditional values."

Hate is hate. You can cover it with self-righteousness and sprinkle it with justification, but it's still hate.

And it doesn't just stay neatly contained in the places we think it belongs. It seeps into everything: how we see strangers, treat people who don't look or believe like us, and how we view ourselves. And if we don't get honest about that?

If we keep letting hate run unchecked, convincing ourselves that it's "just how people are," then we might as well set the world on fire and call it a day.

The Only Real Question: What Are We Going to Do About It?

Hate isn't some abstract concept. It's not just a problem for "other people." It's ours to deal with. And if we keep pretending it's not that bad, if we keep letting the media, politicians, and corporations feed it to us like junk food, then we will be the reason history repeats itself. So, here's the question: Are you going to be another cog in the machine, another person who justifies their version of hate while condemning everyone else's? Or are you going to break the cycle? Because the world doesn't change because we "hope" it will. It changes when we refuse to keep feeding the fire.

Why People Hate (Spoiler: It's Mostly Insecurity and Fear)

Hate is not natural. It's not hardwired into us. It's learned. Conditioned. It's picked up like a bad habit from the people, systems, and environments we grew up in. But at its core, hate almost always comes from two things:

Insecurity - The Roots Of The Bullshit Tree

People who are truly secure in themselves don't waste their time hating others. They don't need to. They're too busy living their damn lives. But insecure people? They need something or someone to direct their self-hate toward. They hate others because it's easier than admitting they don't like themselves. They tear people down because they feel small and powerless. They attack differences because, deep down, they're afraid of what they don't understand.

And instead of doing the hard work of dealing with their insecurities, they project them outward. It's classic psychological deflection. If they can focus on someone else's flaws, they don't have to deal with their own.

Fear – The Most Manipulated Emotion in the World

Hate and fear go hand in hand. People hate what they fear, and they fear what they don't understand. That's why so much hate is rooted in ignorance. The easiest way to make someone hate something is to make them afraid of it first.

And trust me, the people in power know this. They use it against us every single day. Politicians make you fear "the other side," so you'll vote for them. The media feeds you a steady diet of fear so you'll stay engaged (and keep watching their ads). Religious extremists, corporate elites, and power-hungry leaders weaponize fear to keep people divided because the more we hate each other, the less we pay attention to the ones screwing us over.

It's a scam. And too many people are falling for it.

The Bullshit Excuses People Use to Justify Their Hate

Nobody wants to admit they're a hateful person. So, instead, they find ways to rationalize it. They make excuses. They dress it up in fake morality. Here are some of the most common (and infuriating) ones: "It's just my opinion." No, calling an entire group of people less than human is not an "opinion." That's called bigotry. And bigotry isn't a personality trait; it's a choice. "I was raised this way." Cool. You were raised to believe in Santa Claus and grew out of that. What's stopping you from growing out of this? "They're ruining our country/society/cul ture." No, Karen, people just existing in ways that make you uncomfortable isn't "ruining" anything. You're just mad that the world isn't catering to your outdated worldview anymore. "It's not hate, it's just facts." Yes, the classic "I'm just being logical" defense. If your "facts" always lead you to treat people like shit, maybe check your sources. "I don't see color/gen der/sexuality." Oh, so you ignore people's experiences and pretend systemic inequality doesn't exist? Congrats on being part of the problem.

Hate is never about logic. It's about emotion, ego, and a desperate need to feel superior. And until people stop making excuses for it, nothing will change.

How to Rise Above Hate

Here's where people get stuck. They think the only options are to fight hate with more hate, ignore it completely, or "stay out of it."

But there's a third option: reject hate without losing your fire for justice.

Stop Engaging with Willful Ignorance

Some people don't want to learn. They don't want to grow. They don't want a discussion—they want a fight. And you know what? They're not worth your energy. Pick your battles. If someone is genuinely open to a conversation, have it. But if they're looking to argue, walk away. Let them drown in their ignorance. Imagine you're in a swimming pool, just trying to enjoy the water. Then, some guy jumps in, flailing around, screaming that the water isn't wet. You try to explain, calmly and rationally, that, yes, water is, in fact, wet. But he's not listening. He's too busy thrashing, yelling, making waves.

At some point, you've got to realize you're not in a debate. You're in the splash zone of someone wanting to drown in bullshit. And the more you try to save them, the more you get dragged under with them. So, what do you do? You get out of the damn pool. Let them flail. Let them argue with the water. You have better things to do than waste your breath on someone who doesn't want to learn to swim.

Educate Yourself (and Others)

Hate thrives in misinformation. The more you educate yourself, the harder it is for bullshit to take root. Read real history. Listen to different perspectives. Challenge your own biases. And when you see someone spreading false, harmful narratives? Call it out.

Imagine your mind is a garden. If you ignore what's growing, weeds, misinformation, biases, and straight-up lies start creeping in. And hate? Hate is an invasive species. It thrives in neglected spaces, unchecked ignorance, and soil that's never been tilled with new knowledge. Educating yourself is like pulling those weeds before they take over. It's turning over the dirt, planting facts, and watering your understanding with different perspectives. And when you see someone else letting the weeds take over? Hand them a shovel. Show them how to clear the mess. But would they instead sit there, tangled in the overgrowth, refusing to change? That's on them. You can't force someone to tend to their garden, but you don't have to let their weeds spread to yours.

Choose Humanity Over Ego

It's easy to dehumanize people who disagree with you. It's easy to write them off as hopeless. But if we genuinely want to improve the world, we must be better. That doesn't mean tolerating hate; it means refusing to become what we're fighting against. Imagine you're in a burning building. The smoke is thick, the heat is unbearable, and everyone inside is panicking, trying to find a way out. Now, you see someone trapped, coughing, struggling, but instead of helping, you yell, "Well, you're the idiot who lit the match!" and walk away. That's what happens when we let ego take over. It's easy to dehumanize people who think differently, to write them off as lost causes, to decide they're not worth saving. But if the goal is to improve the world, we must improve. That doesn't mean excusing hate or pretending ignorance is harmless; it means refusing to add to the fire. It means choosing to be the one looking for the exits, leading others toward something better instead of standing there, watching it all burn, to prove a point.

Remember That Anger Without Action is Useless

Feeling angry about injustice is normal. But if all you do is rant about it online and scream at people who already agree, that's not change. That's just emotional venting. Donate to causes that fight hate. Support marginalized communities in fundamental ways. Vote for policies that dismantle systemic oppression. Call out injustice when you see it, even when it's uncomfortable.

Imagine you're in a car, flooring the gas pedal but never

taking it out of park. The engine is roaring, the wheels are spinning, but you're not going anywhere. That's what anger without action looks like: loud, exhausting, and ultimately useless. Being mad at injustice is normal. But if all you do is rev your frustration in circles, ranting to people who already agree with you, nothing changes. Real movement requires shifting gears, donating, voting, supporting marginalized communities, and speaking up when uncomfortable. Because if you're not pushing forward, you're just burning fuel and making noise.

Hate is a choice. It's a learned behavior. And the only way to undo it is to actively, intentionally refuse to play the game. If you've been carrying around hate, whether it was taught to you, forced on you, or something you developed along the way, let it go. It's not strength. It's not power. It's poison. And it's only hurting you.

And if you're tired of the world being full of hate, here's the truth: It doesn't change unless people like you change it.

So be that person.

Because you know what hate...well, hates?

Being told to fuck off.

19

CHAPTER 19: COMPASSION: THE SUPERPOWER NO ONE TALKS ABOUT

Compassion gets a bad rap.

People treat it like it's some weak, soft, kumbaya bullshit, like if you're compassionate, you're just some naive little lamb skipping through life, letting people walk all over you. That's not compassion. That's being a doormat. People run from compassion like it's a debt they don't want to owe because once you acknowledge someone's pain, you can't ignore it anymore.

Real compassion? It's a superpower. And it's one of the most complex, substantial, and rebellious things you can practice in a world that thrives on tearing people apart. Because, let's be honest, our world isn't built on empathy right now. It's built on competition. Judgment. Blame. Call-out culture. Everyone's obsessed with proving they're better, smarter, and more right than everyone else. And when people mess up? They're instantly written off, canceled, or shoved into a category of "irredeemable."

Life isn't that black and white. People are complicated. And more often than not, the difference between someone being an absolute dumpster fire of a person and someone getting their shit together comes down to one thing, whether or not they were met with compassion along the way.

And yeah, I know what you're thinking: "Some people don't deserve compassion." "What about toxic people? What about abusers? What about the assholes who don't change?" And you're right; compassion doesn't mean letting people hurt you. It doesn't mean tolerating bullshit. It doesn't mean excusing the inexcusable.

It does mean choosing to see people as human, even when they're at their worst. It means refusing to play the same hate-fueled game that's ruining everything. It means realizing that people are shaped by their experiences, pain, and circumstances, just like you.

And most importantly? It means giving that same grace to yourself.

Because how many times have you held onto shame for something you did when you were struggling? How often do you replay your mistakes, believing they define you? The world is quick to tell people they're too broken, too flawed, too much. But genuine compassion says, you're still here. You're still growing. You're not the worst thing you've ever done.

Compassion is hard. It's uncomfortable. It forces you to hold space for things you don't understand and demands you challenge the knee-jerk reaction to judge, condemn, or write people off.

But if we're serious about changing things, about healing, about becoming better, about breaking the cycles that keep screwing up humanity, compassion has to be part of the equation.

Empathy Is Not Weakness

Somewhere along the way, the world decided that kindness, empathy, and compassion were signs of weakness. Being "tough" meant shutting off your emotions and acting like nothing affects you.

But let me ask you this: who do you think is stronger? A person who builds walls so high they never have to feel anything? Or a person who can stand in front of another human being who is flawed, broken, or even downright unlikable and still chooses to see their humanity? Compassion takes strength. Empathy takes effort. Giving a shit in a world that encourages apathy? That's hard.

You know what's easy? Hate. Judgment. Blame. It takes zero effort to write someone off as a lost cause. It takes no emotional intelligence to decide that because someone is struggling, failing, different, or making bad choices, they're just a "bad person," and that's the end.

But real strength? That comes from looking at someone and saying: "I see you. I disagree with you. I might not even like you. But I see you." "You're more than your worst moment." "You're struggling, and that doesn't mean you're worthless." And yeah, that shit is uncomfortable. Writing people off is more effortless because being angry is so much easier. It's easier not to care.

But compassion isn't about doing what's easy. It's about doing what's right.

The Difference Between Setting Boundaries and Becoming Cold

Compassion does not mean tolerating toxicity. Bullshit needs to be flushed.

There's a vast difference between compassion and letting people walk all over you. Boundaries exist because of compassion.

Think about it: if you don't set boundaries, what happens? You get drained. You get resentful. You start seeing everyone as a problem, and before you know it, you're burned out, bitter, and ready to shut the world out entirely. But when you set boundaries? When you recognize that you can care about people without letting them drag you down? That's when compassion works.

Compassion without boundaries = self-destruction.

Boundaries without compassion = becoming numb.

The goal is balance. You can be kind and firm. You can offer understanding without being a doormat. You can love people without losing yourself in the process. So, when people tell you, "Just cut off anyone who drains you," Nah, it's deeper than that. Some people don't need to be cut off. Some people need to be held at a healthy distance.

And the moment you figure out how to do that?

You unlock a whole new level of peace.

Learning to See People Beyond Their Worst Moments

Let's get real: Everyone has been the villain in someone's story. You. Me. Everyone. We've all said the wrong thing. We've all hurt people, sometimes on purpose, sometimes by accident. We've all had moments we'd take back if we could. And yet, when other people mess up? We act like their worst moment defines them forever. We judge them as if they can never be more than the mistakes they made. We slap a label on them, file them in our mental "irredeemable" folder, and move on.

Don't get it twisted; some people show you who they are and don't deserve a second chance. Some people are toxic, dangerous, or simply unwilling to change. I've met several of these people. But for the vast majority of people? They're just human. And humans are messy.

I learned this the hard way when I was a trooper.

There was this one guy, I'll never forget him. He had been arrested more times than I could count, always for something self-destructive: public intoxication, fights, DUIs. Whenever I came across him, I knew exactly what I was walking into. He was loud, aggressive, and damn near impossible to reason with when he was drunk.

One night, I responded to a call involving him again. Same shit, different day. But this time, something was different. When I walked up, he wasn't screaming. He wasn't belligerent. He was sitting there on the curb, staring at his hands like they held some answer he couldn't find.

For once, I didn't lead with authority. I just sat down next to him.

And in that moment, for the first time, he talked. Not at me.

226

Not through the haze of alcohol. Just talked. About the things he had seen. The losses he never processed. The pain he didn't know how to carry. And I realized this guy wasn't just some repeat offender who wanted to ruin his life. He was drowning in shit no one had ever helped him process. Now, does that mean he didn't have to face consequences? No. Did it mean I excused everything he had done? No. But it did mean I stopped seeing him as just a problem and somebody closer to me than I wanted to admit. He may only have one bad day or decision ahead of me. Maybe my breakdown is right behind his.

Was he a criminal? Yeah, buddy. Did it define him? Maybe you'll get to ask him someday. He's now a manager of a major franchisee.

People aren't their rap sheets. They aren't their worst mistakes. They aren't the total of every bad decision they've ever made.

Compassion doesn't mean ignoring red flags. It doesn't mean pretending people's actions don't have consequences. It doesn't mean you let your guard down all the way. It means recognizing that people can grow. They can learn. They can be more than the worst thing they've ever done. They can be a piece of shit today and save your life tomorrow. Don't forget that.

And if you're thinking, "Yeah, but some people don't change," you're right. Some don't. But that's on them. Your job isn't to fix people. Your job is to choose whether you respond with bitterness or with boundaries. When you start seeing others this way, it changes how you see yourself.

Because if they aren't just the worst thing they've ever done... then maybe, just maybe, neither are you.

The Power of Giving Grace to Yourself and Others

Grace. Patience. Understanding.

Do you ever notice how you're way harsher on yourself than you are on other people? If your best friend made a mistake, you'd probably tell them: "It's okay. You're human. You'll learn from this." But when you mess up? "Wow, I'm a failure. I ruin everything. Why am I like this?" See the problem?

Compassion isn't just about how you treat others. It's about how you treat yourself.

You are going to fuck up. Let's revisit that thought. You are 100% going to fuck up. You are going to make bad choices. You will say things you regret, hurt people unintentionally, and have moments where you feel like the worst person in the world.

And when that happens? You have two choices: Drown in guilt and self-loathing. Or. Take accountability, learn from it, and move forward with self-compassion.

One keeps you stuck. The other lets you grow.

And the more grace you give yourself? The more you'll be able to extend that same grace to others.

Because compassion isn't about being perfect, it's not about excusing bad behavior. It's not about pretending the world isn't full of assholes. It's about choosing to be better than the world expects you to be. It's about refusing to become another angry, bitter, miserable person who treats everyone like shit just because life has been unfair.

It's about realizing how you treat people, including yourself, directly reflects who you are.

Strength in Compassion

If there's one thing to take away from this, it's this: Compassion isn't a weakness. It's strength.

It's one of the hardest things to practice in a world that runs on outrage, blame, and self-righteousness. It's easy to tear people down. It's easy to assume the worst. It's easy to write people off and decide they don't deserve another chance.

But compassion? That takes real strength. It's having the guts to see the good in people, even when it's hard. It's setting boundaries without losing your ability to care. It's choosing understanding over judgment. It's giving yourself grace when you need it. And in a world that seems more divided, more hateful, and more broken than ever? Compassion is rebellion.

Think about it. Everything around you is designed to make you pick a side, to make you see people as "us" or "them, " to make you believe that some people are worth caring about and others just...aren't. Social media thrives on division. Politics weaponizes it. Friendships and families break apart because people would rather be right than compassionate.

But let's be honest: most people don't even know why they hate the people they hate. They were taught to. They absorbed it. They've convinced themselves that their version of anger, resentment, and dismissal is justified. And every time they double down on that narrative, they become another pawn in a system that wants us divided.

Compassion, though? That flips the whole game on its head. Because compassion isn't about letting people off the hook, it's not about being naïve. It's about fully seeing people— flaws and all, and still refusing to dehumanize them. And yeah, some people will call that weak. They'll say it's soft.

They'll mistake kindness for being passive. But the truth? Compassion is dangerous to a system that thrives on hate.

Do you know what takes real strength? Not reacting with the same bitterness the world throws at you, holding your boundaries without turning cold and detached, standing in your truth without shoving someone else down to prove your point, and having the audacity to believe that people can change—even when it's easier to write them off.

But the most challenging part? Turning that same compassion inward.

Because the truth is, most people who struggle to give grace to others are the same people who don't know how to give it to themselves. The ones who are hardest on you? They're probably just as brutal to themselves in their head. The ones who judge the loudest? They probably can't stand the parts of themselves that look too much like what they claim to hate.

And if that's you, if you've spent your whole life beating yourself up for every mistake, every flaw, every way you think you've fallen short, then you are exactly who needs this the most. Compassion is about looking at yourself, in all your messiness, all your imperfections, all your regrets, and saying, "Yeah, I've screwed up. But I'm still here. And I'm still worthy."

Because that's what strength is. Not anger. Not judgment. Not bitterness disguised as a moral high ground.

Strength is choosing to be better when the world expects you to be worse.

It's saying I don't have to be like the others.

I can choose to love because it's right or to hate because it's popular.

But to me, there's no choice. Hate doesn't get to win.

20

CHAPTER 20: KINDNESS – THE MOST REBELLIOUS THING YOU CAN DO

Similar to empathy and compassion, kindness is not a weakness.

I don't know who started this rumor that being kind means being soft, naive, or quickly taken advantage of, but they've got it all wrong. Somewhere along the way, people started equating kindness with passivity, like if you're a decent human being, you must also let people walk all over you. For example, if you choose kindness, you're somehow weak. Like if you refuse to be an asshole, you must be easy to manipulate.

Hell no.

Kindness is not rolling over and letting the world kick you in the ribs. It's not tolerating toxic people. It's not saying "yes" when you want to scream "no." And it's not letting other people's bullshit go unchecked to "keep the peace."

Kindness isn't cowardice; it's courage.

It takes strength to be kind in a world that's trained people to be guarded, skeptical, and ruthless. It's easy to be an asshole. It's easy to build walls so high that nobody can get close enough to hurt you. Becoming cold, cynical, and detached is easy because it feels safer than risking vulnerability.

But kindness? That takes guts. Being kind is standing up for what's right, even when uncomfortable. Being kind is setting boundaries, even when people don't like it. Kindness treats people respectfully, even when they don't return the favor. Being kind is knowing that you don't have to turn into an asshole just because the world has been cruel to you.

I've seen this play out in real life. I've worked with people who have been hurt so severely that their first instinct is to shut down, shut out, and build an emotional fortress no one can get through. They're afraid that if they show an ounce of softness, they'll be taken advantage of again.

And honestly? I get it.

Because kindness is risky, it means opening yourself up to the possibility of someone taking advantage of it. That someone will mistake it for weakness. That someone will try to use it against you. But here's what people don't get: kindness is not about them. It's about you. It's about the kind of person you want to be. It's about refusing to let the worst experiences of your life turn you into something you're not. It's about staying human when the world wants to turn you into stone.

Kindness doesn't mean you let people use you. It means you refuse to become like those who tried to break you. So, if you've ever thought, "I can't be kind because people will take advantage of me," understand this: you can be kind without being a pushover. You can be compassionate without being naïve. You can be understanding without being a doormat.

Kindness and strength aren't opposites. They're the same

damn thing.

The Ripple Effect of Small, Intentional Kindness

We've all seen those corny motivational posters about how "one act of kindness can change the world." And let's be honest, it's easy to roll your eyes at that kind of sentiment when the world feels like it's going to shit.

But it's true. Not in some magical, fairy-tale, world-peace kind of way. But in an honest, measurable, undeniable way. Think about the last time a stranger did something unexpectedly kind for you. Maybe they paid for your coffee. Maybe they let you merge into traffic when everyone else was being a road-raging asshole (like I usually am). Perhaps they held the door open when you were carrying too much shit.

It was a small thing. Barely worth mentioning. And yet, for a split second, it changed your entire mood. It reminded you that not everyone in the world sucks. It made you feel seen. It made you feel lighter, even if just for a moment. That's the power of kindness.

When you experience real, intentional, genuine kindness, it has a way of spreading. You're more likely to pass it on when someone makes you feel good. You're more likely to hold the door for the next person, let someone else merge, or say something kind when you could've just stayed silent.

And suddenly? That small moment of kindness isn't tiny anymore. It's a chain reaction. It's a shift.

And in a world running on cruelty, division, and selfishness? That shift matters.

How Choosing Kindness Disrupts Hate

If you want to piss people off, try being kind to someone they think doesn't deserve it. Seriously. Nothing confuses or enrages people more than unexpected, undeserved kindness. The world has trained us to believe in a system of transactional morality, that people should only be treated well if they've "earned" it. That respect is conditional. That kindness should be withheld as punishment for bad behavior. And sure, there are absolutely people who don't deserve your time, energy, or emotional investment—but withholding kindness to prove a point? That doesn't make you powerful. That makes you petty.

The actual rebellion is in refusing to play the game at all. Kindness is disruptive. It dismantles anger. It confuses people who expect hostility. It takes the fuel out of the fire. Imagine you are trying to fight someone, and they say, "That shirt brings out the ocean blue in your eyes." Your brain is going to be like, what? Wait? Thank you...But hit you? No...nice thing. Mad?

Kindness doesn't mean tolerating hate. It doesn't mean you let bigots spew their bullshit without calling them out. It doesn't mean you "turn the other cheek" when someone actively harms you or others. But it means you don't let their hate dictate who you are. Because if you start responding to hate with more hate, guess what? They win. The people who thrive on division, rage, and cruelty want you to match their energy. They want you to lower yourself to their level. They want you to abandon your humanity to prove a point.

And when you don't? When you refuse to become what they want you to be? Money can't buy that drug.

234

Being Kind in a World That Doesn't Always Deserve It

Can we be kind in a world that doesn't deserve it? In a world this fucking exhausting?

People can be selfish. People can be cruel. People can be ignorant, hateful, and unapologetically awful. And it's easy to look at all that and think, Why should I even bother? Why should I be kind when the world isn't kind to me? Why should I be decent when everyone else is just out for themselves? Why should I care when nobody else seems to?

Because the alternative is worse.

If you let the world's ugliness turn you bitter, angry, and closed off, the world wins. You don't have to be kind because people deserve it. You don't have to be kind because it'll always be returned. You don't have to be kind because it's easy to do.

You must be kind because the world desperately needs people who refuse to let it harden them.

Because kindness is what keeps us human; it's what keeps us connected. It's what keeps us from turning into the very thing we hate. So no, you don't have to be kind to everyone. You don't have to extend kindness to people who continually disrespect you. You don't have to put yourself in harm's way to be "nice."

But you can choose kindness as an act of rebellion. You can choose kindness as a way to protect your soul.

You can choose kindness not because the world deserves it but because you deserve a world where kindness exists.

And if that world doesn't exist yet?

Then, it's up to us to build it.

The Strength in Kindness

Kindness is about strength. It's about resistance. It's about choice. You can be kind and still set boundaries. You can be kind and still stand up for yourself. You can be kind and still hold people accountable. Because genuine kindness? It's not just "niceness." It's not surface-level politeness.

It's control. It's controlling the narrative. It's the control to change your environment to better fit you and others. It's power. It's the power to shape the world into something better. It's the power to disrupt hate. It's the power to remind people that light still exists even in the darkest places.

And in a world that keeps telling you to be selfish, cruel, and cynical?

Be kind. It hates that.

21

CHAPTER 21: SO, WHO ARE YOU? NOW?

Alright, we've torn through the bullshit. We've dismantled the lies. We've exposed the programming. We've kicked down the doors of every system, expectation, and belief that tried to box you in, keep you small, and dictate who you were allowed to be. Now it's time for the real question. It's not the question society has been trying to answer for you. Not the question your parents, your peers, your culture, or your trauma have been whispering in your ear. Not the question fear has been screaming at you every time you thought about stepping outside the lines.

The only question that matters: Who are you going to be? Not the person you were told to be. Not the person you thought you had to be to survive. Not the version of you that played it safe and shrank to fit or morphed into whatever made other people comfortable. You. The real you. The one beneath all the conditioning gets to rise now that the weight of expectation has been stripped away. The one who finally understands just how much power you have over your life.

Burn the Old Blueprint—Build Your Own

You've realized something crucial by now: you don't have to keep living a life that others designed. You don't have to follow some outdated checklist that someone else decided was the measure of a "successful" human being. You don't have to keep playing a role just because it's familiar, just because it's what you've always done, just because it makes other people comfortable. You don't have to drag your old identity into your future if it doesn't serve you anymore.

So, we're going to burn that old blueprint to the ground. The expectations? Gone. The people-pleasing? Ashes. The guilt for not being who they wanted you to be? Fucking vaporized. Because the truth is, your identity was never meant to be static. You are not a monument to your past, frozen in place, trapped in the choices and labels handed to you. You are a work in progress, a constantly evolving force. And now? Now, you get to build something entirely new. Something real. Something free. Something that is yours.

The Most Important Decision You'll Ever Make

This isn't about "finding yourself." That's a cute phrase, but you're not some lost sock in the dryer. You're not missing. You're right here. You always have been. You've just been buried under expectations, under fear, under versions of yourself that were never yours but felt easier to wear because they kept the peace, made other people comfortable, and were what you thought you had to be.

But here's the truth: You don't need to find yourself. You need

238

to unearth yourself. To peel back the layers of conditioning, guilt, and outdated identities that no longer fit. So instead of asking, Who am I? start asking: Who do I want to become? What kind of life excites me? What version of me feels the most alive? What do I need to start doing? What do I need to stop tolerating? Because identity isn't something you stumble upon. It's something you create. Every choice, boundary, and decision to step into who you are is you, laying the foundation, brick by brick.

And the best part? You're the architect. The blueprint is yours to design. No limits. No rules. Just you, finally building the life that was meant to be yours.

The Freedom (and Fear) of Self-Definition

The wildest part of breaking free from society's expectations is that, for the first time, you are fully responsible for who you become. No more scripts. No more pre-approved paths. Just you, standing face-to-face with the reality that your life, choices, identity, and future are entirely in your hands. That's both terrifying and liberating. No more hiding behind, "This is just who I am." No more blaming your circumstances, your past, or the people who tried to mold you into something smaller than you were meant to be. No more waiting for permission to exist as your most authentic, most whole self. Because now? Now, it's all on you.

And yeah, that kind of accountability might scare the shit out of you. It should. Because for the first time, there's no one left to make the call but you. There is no system to lean on. There is no excuse to fall back on. Just the raw, undeniable truth that you are in the driver's seat of your own life. But here's the thing: that's what freedom looks like. It's not just breaking the chains; it's stepping up and deciding where you go next. It's scary because it's real. Because there's no more autopilot.

Write Your Own Damn Story

Most people spend their lives following a blueprint they never designed, ticking off boxes they didn't choose, chasing a version of success someone else defined, and staying in lines they never dared to question. They convince themselves that this is just how life works and how things are done, even if it feels empty or wrong.

Enough of that.

At all moments of your life, it belongs to you. Who you were isn't the boss of who you're becoming. You don't have to wear a label that no longer fits. You don't have to keep holding onto a past version of yourself just because it's what people expect. Identities aren't set in stone; you weren't born to be one thing forever.

So, who are you going to be? The person who stays stuck in a life that doesn't fulfill them? Or the person who chooses to build something real? The person who plays small, afraid to step outside the lines? Or the person who refuses to be boxed in? The person who lets the world define them? Or the person who stands up and says, "No, this time, I decide."

Shred the old script. Smash the rules. Take the wheel like you own the road.

22

CHAPTER 22: THE S.H.I.F.T. SHOW – IT'S UNCOMFORTABLE. IT'S WORTH IT.

You've been introduced to the S.H.I.F.T. Framework™. Here's where we break it down and determine its use in your life.

This is where you either pretend you didn't read any of this book, and go back to the same cycles that have been kicking your ass for years.

This is the make-or-break moment. Awareness is great. Understanding the chaos around you? That's important. Digging into your trauma, grief, mental health, cultural conditioning, and self-worth? That's necessary. But none of it means shit if you don't do something with it. You could highlight every page of this book, send quotes to your friends, and nod along like, "Wow, this is deep." But you're wasting your time if you're not ready to act. You paid money for this book. Use its words to invest in your own damn life.

And I know what you're thinking.

"But change is hard. But I don't know where to start. But

what if I fail? But what if it's uncomfortable?" Yeah. It's gonna be hard. It's gonna be uncomfortable. And you're probably gonna fail a few times. That's part of it. But so what?

What's the alternative? Stay in the same patterns that make you miserable? Keep waiting for life to fix itself magically? Let your past, your pain, or other people dictate your entire future?

Because that's the choice you're making if you do nothing.

Look, I get it. Taking control of your life is terrifying. It's much easier to stay in the familiar, even if the familiar sucks. It's easier to blame circumstances, let your past be a permission slip for your present, and tell yourself you'll change "someday."

But let me ask you, how many times have you already said "someday"? How often have you thought about changing, dreamt about changing, and promised yourself you'd change... only to stay precisely where you are? How many years have you wasted waiting?

Because here's the truth no one wants to hear; you don't get unlimited chances to figure this out. You don't get to press pause on life and hope that things magically realign while you sit there waiting for the perfect moment.

You either choose to take the wheel, or you stay stuck in the same predictable loop, same thoughts, same fears, same excuses, same damn life.

You're either in control, or you're just another passenger on the bullshit train.

So, what's it gonna be?

Stay or S.H.I.F.T.?

The S.H.I.F.T. Blueprint: The Only Way Out Is Through

I didn't create this self-help acronym to look cute on a vision board. I created it for you to apply to your life in the ways that help you specifically.

This is the five-part blueprint for taking your power back, cutting the excuses, and finally doing what needs to be done. And it starts with the most challenging part, stopping the shit that's keeping you where you don't want to be.

S: STOP - Cut the Bullshit & Quit Giving Power to What Doesn't Serve You

First things first, what do you need to quit? Quit waiting for someone to save you. Quit explaining yourself to people who don't even understand themselves. Quit tolerating relationships, jobs, habits, and mindsets that are draining you. Quit feeding the drama, the negativity, the self-doubt, and the fear. You don't need a new plan. You don't need more time. You don't need to wait for the "right moment." You need to STOP doing the shit that's actively keeping you miserable. Are you constantly exhausted, overwhelmed, and stretched too thin? STOP over-committing to shit that doesn't matter. STOP putting other people's needs before your own 100% of the time. STOP running yourself into the ground like some people-pleasing martyr.

Are you stuck in a job you hate but never make moves to change it? STOP convincing yourself that it's "too late" to switch things up. STOP making excuses about "security" while ignoring that you're slowly dying inside and still dealing with toxic people in your life. STOP pretending they'll change when they've shown you, repeatedly, who they are. STOP keeping people around just because of history, guilt, or obligation. Stopping isn't passive. It's a decision. It's looking at your life and saying, "Nope. Not this. Not anymore."

If you never stop feeding the bullshit, the bullshit will never stop bullshitting you.

H: HYPE – Pump Yourself Up & Take the Damn Lead

You're the main character of your life. Start acting like it.

Hype isn't about arrogance. It's about self-respect. It's about looking in the mirror and backing yourself the fuck up. Stop talking to yourself like you're a failure. Stop acting like you're lucky to be in the rooms you worked your ass off to be in. Stop downplaying your wins, your strengths, your existence.

If you don't hype yourself up, who the hell will? You've got a dream, but you're scared you're not "good enough." Well, guess what? Nobody starts out being good. Confidence isn't something you're born with—it's built through action. You struggle to set boundaries because you don't want to "seem mean." Newsflash: Protecting your peace doesn't mean it's necessary. You can be a kind person and still not put up with bullshit. The fix? Start acting like you matter. Speak up. Take up space. Show up in your own life.

Hype yourself up. And if it feels weird at first? Good. That means you're finally doing it right.

I: INNOVATE – Reinvent How You Approach Life

The old way? It's broken. The old rules? They weren't made for you. The old mindset? It's keeping you small. The old systems? They're built to keep people trapped. So why the hell are you still following them? You hate the 9-5 grind, but assume it's your only option. It's not. Innovate. Create your damn path. People make a living reviewing snacks on TikTok. There is no "one way" to succeed anymore. You've been stuck in the same unhealthy patterns forever. Well, what if you approached things completely differently? New habits, new environments, new strategies. If what you're doing isn't working, change it. You think success looks a certain way because society says so. Innovate your version. Define success on your terms.

If you don't like the game, stop playing.

F: FIGHT – Stand Your Ground & Stop Letting Life Steamroll You

This is the part where you stop taking shit. From the world. From other people. From yourself.

Fight for your boundaries. Fight for your goals. Fight for the version of yourself that refuses to settle. Do you feel like life keeps knocking you down? That's normal. But do you stay down, or do you get back up? That's the fight. People around you don't support your growth? Too bad. Grow anyway. They were never really in your corner if they can't handle it. Are you scared of failure? Good. That means you care. The fight isn't about never failing but not quitting when you do.

T: THRIVE – Live Unapologetically on Your Damn Terms

This is what it's all for—not just surviving and not just making it through. Thriving. And it looks different to everyone. But the one thing it's NOT? Living according to someone else's expectations. Thriving might mean peace, cutting out the noise, and choosing happiness over hustle. Thriving might mean freedom, breaking out of systems that don't serve you. Thriving might mean impact, doing work that matters to you. You decide.

Bridging the Chaos to the S.H.I.F.T.

If you've stuck around this long, chances are you've had a few wake-up calls, a couple of gut punches, some hard-to-swallow truths, and maybe even a holy shit, I've been living a damn lie, moment. We've gone deep into the chaos, how the world keeps people stuck, how we keep ourselves stuck, and how most of us are walking around on autopilot, wondering why nothing ever changes.

Knowing all this and understanding how we've been conditioned, manipulated, and held back means nothing if you don't do something about it. This is the part where people usually look for an out. They say, "I get it, but maybe I'm the exception. Maybe I'm not that stuck. Maybe things will get better on their own."

Let me be blunt: they won't. Nothing changes if nothing changes. Life is not Netflix; stop sitting around for the next season to drop and film your show! (Don't make that weird.) (You made it weird.) (It's funny now.)

So, cut through the bullshit and discover what happens when

you decide to S.H.I.F.T.

"Later" Is An Illusion

Later isn't real. It represents a time that hasn't happened yet. An unknown realm yet to unfold. It's the universe's junk drawer where good intentions go to die. It's saving a seat on a bus that hasn't arrived yet. It's the ghost of productivity.

Most people don't refuse to change. They tell themselves they'll do it later. "I'll start next Monday." "After the holidays, things will slow down, and I'll have time." "Once I get through this stressful phase, I'll focus on myself."

Later is a lie.

You don't suddenly wake up one day with the perfect conditions for change. Life doesn't roll out a red carpet for you and say, "Alright, now's a great time to reinvent yourself." You either make the shift now, in the middle of the mess, the chaos, and the uncertainty, or you never will. Because comfort zones? They expand. They stretch to fit every excuse you feed them until suddenly; you've been sitting in the same place for ten years, convincing yourself you need more time.

Why Change Feels So Damn Hard

There's a reason your brain always goes back to what it knows: what's safe, what's understood, and what's familiar. It's not wired for change. It's wired for safety. And safety, to your brain, means predictability. Even if your current life is making you miserable, draining you, or actively screwing you over, your brain still thinks, Yeah, but at least we know what to expect here.

Change, on the other hand. Unknown. Unfamiliar. Risky.

So, the second you shift, your brain freaks out.

It'll whisper: "Are you sure you can handle this?" (Translation: Let's return to the old way, Which was more manageable.) "What if you fail?" (Translation: If you never try, you'll never have to deal with disappointment.) "You're being dramatic. Your life isn't that bad." (Translation: Stay small. Stay stuck. Stay comfortable.)

This is the inner war, the battle between the part of you that wants more and the part of you that would rather keep things familiar, even if familiar sucks.

Most People Quit Right Here

Most people who try to change hit this wall and say, "Welp, I guess I'm just not meant to be different." They take the resistance as a sign to stop. But resistance proves you're doing something right. If you feel uncomfortable, if your old habits are pulling at you like quicksand, if your mind is begging you to go back to how things were, that means you're on the edge of a breakthrough.

This is where most people quit. This is where you won't.

Because the only way to make it through this phase is to expect it, embrace it, and push through it.

The Turning Point: When You Push Through

Let's say you push past this resistance. You ignore the fear, the self-doubt, the urge to slide back into old patterns. You keep moving forward. At first? It still feels weird. You're rewiring yourself, breaking free from old thought patterns, challenging ingrained beliefs, and forcing yourself to see the world (and yourself) differently.

But then something shifts.

One day, you wake up and realize that you don't react the same way to things that used to trigger you. You don't feel like you're drowning in your mind anymore. You don't tolerate the same bullshit you used to. You don't let fear make decisions for you.

This is when the S.H.I.F.T. stops being a concept and becomes your reality.

The Question You Have to Answer

Here are your options.

Behind door #1: You stay the same. You keep living the way you have been. You keep waiting for "later." You keep telling yourself that one-day things will magically get better.

Behind door #2: You S.H.I.F.T. You face the resistance head-on. You get uncomfortable. You push through. You reclaim your life. One road is easy, but it leads nowhere. The other road is hard but leads to everything you want.

So.

Which path are you taking?

Because whether you realize it or not, you're already making a choice.

The S.H.I.F.T. Framework™: The Real-World Stories That Built It

Now that we've crossed the breaking point let's get honest about where this whole S.H.I.F.T. framework came from.

Because I didn't just wake up one day, sip my coffee, and say, "Hey, you know what sounds cool? A five-step, potentially life-changing philosophy." Is that a stretch? Your choice.

Nope. This framework was built in the trenches. It was constructed from real-life experiences, from watching people succeed and self-destruct, jobs that drained me, losses that broke me, and moments that changed me forever. This isn't a theory. It's real-life shit.

I've seen what happens when people stay stuck. I've seen what happens when people decide to shift. And before we go breaking down each step of S.H.I.F.T. further, I need you to know why it exists.

Because every letter in this framework? It has a story. It's been lived. It's constantly being tested and continually being proven. Some of you may have already been shifting in your way. This way, however, isn't some "feel-good, manifest-your-way-to-success" BS. This is what works when life has kicked your ass, when your mind has turned against you, and when the weight of everything feels impossible to lift. And if you're thinking, "Yeah, but my situation is different," let me stop you right there.

Before this framework existed, its components were alive and well all around us. People shift their lives every day. Maybe you were already on your journey, and this book is just another push in the right direction. With a few more cuss words, of course. Still on the cussing thing?

250

I've seen people who had nothing, no support, no hope, no belief in themselves, completely rebuild their existence. I've seen people seconds away from giving up find a way to fight back. And I've been there myself.

So, before we start breaking it down step by step, let's talk about how each piece was built through real moments, real people, and real lessons that hit hard.

Because if you don't understand where this came from, you won't know why it matters.

And trust me, it matters.

S: Stop – The Moment You Realize You're Stuck

A certain kind of soul-crushing exhaustion comes from living a life that isn't yours. It's not just about hating your job or feeling unfulfilled. It's deeper than that. It's waking up every day with a low-grade dread in your stomach because you know, deep down, that this isn't where you're supposed to be. It's clocking in and out of your existence, feeling like a side character in someone else's story.

I saw this when I worked at a pizza place as a teenager.

Have you ever met someone who's completely given up but still goes through the motions of life? That was some of my coworkers. They'd been there for years, taking orders, throwing dough, standing in the same spot, doing the same thing, like their lives were a VHS tape stuck on repeat. Is that a sad existence? Was that person happy, living on their terms, and thriving? If so. Throw that dough! That wasn't the case.

They hated it.

They complained every single shift. They dreamed out loud about better lives, jobs, and opportunities. And yet, they never left. And you know what scared me? I saw how easy it was to become them. To get comfortable in the discomfort. To wake up five years later and realize, "Shit, I never actually left."

The Loudest Regret: The Nursing Home Realization

I saw the same thing when I worked in a nursing home. Except this time? The regret was louder. Thicker. More controlling. Because these weren't just people stuck in a lousy job. These were people at the end of their lives. And do you know what I heard more than anything else? "I wish I had..." Not "I'm glad I stayed safe." Not "I'm proud of how cautious I was." Not "I'm glad I never took the risk." But: "I wish I had taken more chances." "I wish I had told them how I felt." "I wish I had done something that scared me." "I wish I had lived for myself instead of for everyone else."

Imagine sitting in a wheelchair, staring out a window at a world you're no longer a part of, realizing that you played it safe for decades... and now you're out of time.

That's the kind of regret that haunts you.

That's the kind of realization that hits too late.

We don't have to end up there. We may still find ourselves in a nursing home, but we don't have to be disappointed in the life that led us there.

Why STOP is the First Step

If you don't stop and look at where your life is heading, you will wake up one day in a place you were never meant to be.

And not just physically. Mentally. Emotionally. Financially. One day turns into a year. A year turns into a decade. And before you know it? Your entire life has been written by decisions you never consciously made. That's why STOP is the first step. Because if you don't stop, you don't notice when you're getting stuck. If you don't stop, you don't realize when you're repeating cycles that no longer serve you. If you don't stop, you don't see the exit signs before you pass them.

So, ask yourself: Am I happy with my direction? Am I making choices, or am I just letting life happen to me? If I keep doing what I'm doing for the next five years, will I be proud of where I end up? If the answer isn't a hell yes, then guess what?

It's time to STOP.

H: Hype – Because If You Don't Believe in You, No One Else Will

Let's talk about self-worth.

Because here's the truth: nobody teaches you to believe in yourself. They tell you to be confident. They ask you to "believe in yourself." They slap motivational quotes on posters and act like that's enough to rewire your brain magically. But they don't tell you how the hell you're supposed to do that. How to drown out the doubt. How to push through fear. How do you convince yourself you're capable when everything in you is screaming otherwise?

Because nobody teaches this, most people default to the most straightforward option and talk themselves out of everything before they even try.

The Two Types of People I've Met in School

College is where I've seen both sides of this coin. Both on campus and online.

Some people had zero belief in themselves and talked themselves out of opportunities, friendships, relationships, and success before they even had a chance. They'd say, "I'm not smart enough for this." "I don't belong here." "What if I fail?" And guess what? They struggled. Not because they weren't capable. Not because they didn't have potential. But they had already decided they weren't good enough before they started.

Then there were the people who hyped themselves up. These weren't necessarily the smartest, the most talented, or the most qualified. But they had one thing that set them apart: audacity. They faced the same challenges and said, "I'll figure it out." They weren't any more experienced but had the confidence to act like they were. They bet on themselves, even when unsure if they could pull it off.

They were the ones who succeeded. Not because they had it all figured out. Not because they had some secret advantage.

But they hyped themselves up because they believed in their ability to figure it out along the way.

Confidence Isn't Magic—It's a Skill

There's this myth that people believe about confidence. They think you either have it or you don't.

Some people are just born charismatic, fearless, and self-assured, while others are doomed to doubt themselves forever. That's not how it works. Confidence isn't something you're born with; it's something you build. Like a muscle. And if you've never worked that muscle? It's gonna feel weak at first. But the more you use, test, and push it, the stronger it gets.

I'll never forget telling my mother I was trying out for the high school basketball team. You see, I was a stud on my junior high squad! There were like eight of us. And there were only fifteen kids in the entire class. No, I'm not kidding. Though I performed well in a small sample size, my mother was justifiably concerned about my five-nine whiteness and its unlikely translation to being chosen for the team. She tried to soften the inevitable blow of failure. But I told her, "I'm making the team." I came home to one of my favorite dinners and a mother eagerly waiting to be the soft place to land for her heartbroken child. She asked how it went, and I told her I had practice on Monday.

Confidence and limitations are like two fighters in the same ring; one is trying to push forward while the other is trying to hold you back. The catch? Your limitations only win if you believe they're stronger than you. Confidence isn't the absence of constraints; it's the refusal to be ruled by them. When you embrace confidence, limitations become stepping stones instead of roadblocks. They are like weights in a gym; one tests your strength, and the other builds it. The more you push against your limits, the stronger your confidence grows.

If You Don't Hype Yourself Up, Who Will?

If you don't believe in yourself, why should anyone else? If you walk into a room like you don't belong there, people will treat you like you don't. If you present yourself as not worth much, people will believe you. The world isn't going to hand you confidence on a silver platter. Nobody is coming to permit you to believe in yourself.

You have to decide right now, today, that you're done waiting for validation. Because self-worth isn't about proving anything to anyone else; it's about looking in the mirror and saying: "I'm the main character in my own life, and I'm gonna act like it." "I might not have all the answers, but I trust myself to figure them out." "I am worth more than the doubts in my head."

And guess what? The second you start acting like you belong in the room, people will start treating you like you do, and eventually, the room will be yours. Not in an ownership of the people in it kind of way, but an ownership of who you are among them sort of way.

So, if you're waiting for permission to start believing in yourself?

Here it is.

I: Innovate – Breaking Out of Broken Systems

Working in a gas station was a weirdly philosophical time in my life. It was there I started questioning my thoughts and beliefs. I grew up in a tiny community of primarily wonderful people right before and after the internet. But it is a small community. Meaning most of us saw the world very similarly. In today's world, it's nearly impossible to agree on anything. I was surrounded by people with the same ideologies—ideas about life and its congruence with the universe. Until I worked at a gas station in the next town; when you work in a gas station in a touristy, beautiful part of the country that just so happens to fall between two exits off of Interstate 81, you meet every walk of life, at every stage of life, with all the problems of life, with no answers to life.

It was in all of these people that I started to see how bullshit the rules are. And not just mildly annoying rules, like "no shirt, no service." I'm talking about deep, ingrained, life-defining bullshit, the kind that keeps people stuck in cycles they don't even realize they're trapped in. People work 85 hours weekly for table scraps, while others spend hundreds of dollars daily on lottery tickets. Watching people limp around because they can't afford to fix what ails them. People are dragging themselves into another mundane, soul-sucking existence. I could see it on their faces. They wanted to be somewhere else. Anywhere else. Some of them wanted to be anybody else.

Here's what most don't realize behind a gas station counter. I saw most of these people every day. I watched their lives unfold in front of me like a poorly filmed but always interesting Hallmark movie. I felt their pain. I heard their stories. I celebrated their victories. I knew them personally without ever seeing them beyond the pumps. It was here that I learned to see people. To really and truly see them. To see how life, in all its various forms of fuckery, influenced and, at times, even dictated their very existence. For many of them, I watched their stories until they ended. The old ladies who one day didn't wave at me from pump two asking for help. One gentleman even requested that I visit him practically on his deathbed because he said, "he was always kind to me."

I saw the people who would return for another case of beer because the first didn't entirely act like the mental Novocain they expected it to. Every day, I watched the same people live the same life repeatedly. People who had been working the same job for decades, hating it, complaining about it, but never leaving. People who spend their entire paychecks on lottery tickets hoping luck will save them instead of themselves. People who had resigned themselves to fate, accepting that "this is just how life is," as if their story had already been written for them.

It was autopilot living. Nobody questioned the system. Nobody stopped and thought, "Wait, do I even want this life I'm living?" They just followed the script. To work, pay your bills, complain about your problems, and repeat.

Seeing the Cycle from the Inside: My Time as a Detention Officer

If the gas station showed me what happens when people stay stuck, working as a detention officer in a regional jail showed me what happens when people get trapped. When you don't innovate and don't find a way to escape broken systems, you don't just stay in one place; you get caught in a downward spiral. I watched people repeat the same mistakes, not because they were stupid, but because they had been taught that failure was their only option.

People who had been in and out of the system since they were kids because nobody gave them an alternative path. People who had been told they were nothing their whole lives so they believed it and acted accordingly. People who couldn't see a future beyond survival because when your entire existence has been about just getting through the day, dreaming about a better life feels like a joke.

It was like watching people fight against an invisible force field. No matter how badly they wanted out, they kept getting pulled back in by how they were raised, their environments, and the belief that this was just how life worked. But here's the truth most people don't want to admit: The system is designed to keep you trapped.

You're handed a script the second you're old enough to understand the world. Go to school. Get a job. Pay your bills. Work for 40 years. If you're lucky, retire before your body gives out. Die. And if that's the life you want? Great. But for a lot of people, it's not. And yet, they follow the script anyway. Why? Because that's what they were told to do. Because breaking the script feels riskier than following it.

Because it's easier to accept a "meh" life than to risk everything for something better.

If You Want a Different Life, You Have to Think Differently

At some point, you must stop and ask yourself: Who made the rules you're following? Because if you never question the script, you'll spend your entire life living out somebody else's story. That's what innovation is about. Not just reinventing how you work. Not just finding a new career or a new mindset.

It's about looking at your life and saying: "What if I stopped playing by the rules that were never meant for me?" "What if I challenged everything I was taught about success, happiness, and purpose?" "What if I stopped following a system that only benefits the people at the top?"

If you want to improve, you must stop following a script that was never made for you. You have to innovate. You must decide your life is yours to build, not theirs to dictate.

F: Fight – Because Life Won't Hand You Shit

If there's one universal truth about life, it's this: You will be tested. Over and over and over again. You will be knocked down. You will be told you're not good enough. You will hit walls so hard it feels like there's no way around them. And when that moment comes, when the pressure is on, and the weight of everything is crushing you into the ground, you have a choice.

Fight or fold.

Seeing the Fight-or-Flight Response in Real Time

Of course, the Fight in S.H.I.F.T. comes from working in law enforcement. No. Not in the sense of some people's irrational belief that all cops are just out here looking to hurt people. That's bullshit. Yes, some people should never wear a badge. But the truth is that most cops would gladly sacrifice themselves to save you. The fight comes from viewing the world behind the windshield of a patrol car. Sometimes it's beautiful. Other times, it erodes your spirit. This is where I saw fight or flight play out in real-time.

Because resilience is one thing to talk about in theory, it's another thing to watch people break right before you. I saw people who crumbled under pressure. People who let fear paralyze them. People who collapsed at the first sign of adversity. And then I saw people who fought. People who had every reason to quit but didn't. People who had been knocked down many times but still got back up. People who stood their ground even when everything was stacked against them.

That's when it hit me: life doesn't care who you are. It

260

doesn't matter how prepared you are. It doesn't care how much you've been through. It doesn't matter whether you're ready for what's coming.

Because life will test you, whether you like it or not.

The Difference Between Fighters and Those Who Fold

I saw two types of people in high-stress situations. The ones who folded. They let fear make their decisions for them. They gave up before they even tried. They told themselves it was "too much" and backed down. The ones who fought. They didn't wait to "feel ready." They acted even when they were scared. They refused to let the situation define them. It wasn't about strength. It wasn't about who had the most training, the most talent, or the most experience. It was about who refused to quit. That's it.

That was the difference between those who rose above the most challenging moments of their lives and those who let those moments define them.

Fighting for Yourself When No One Else Will

Here's the part nobody likes to admit: No one is coming to save you. Not your family. Not your job. Not the government. Not some magical moment of "readiness" that will suddenly make everything easier. If you want to win this fight? You must fight for yourself because nobody will give you a better life.

Nobody will say, "Hey, I noticed you've been struggling. Here's a fast pass out of all your problems." The people who wait for that moment? The people who hope life will get easier?

261

They stay stuck. Forever.

But the people who get up and fight, no matter how many times they get knocked down?

Those are the people who change their story.

You Don't Always Get to Choose What Happens to You—But You Do Get to Choose Whether You Fight or Surrender

Life is unfair. Period. Some people get dealt a better hand than others. Some people face challenges they never asked for. Some people have to fight battles they never should have had to fight. But here's the deal: you don't always get to choose what happens to you. You only get to choose how you respond. Will you let life break you? Or will you stand up and push back?

That's your call. And if you're reading this, if you've made it this far, if something in you knows you're capable of more, then let this be the moment you decide to fight.

Because the world will try to break you.

And your job?

It is to make damn sure it doesn't succeed.

T: Thrive – The Moment You Realize You Made It

Thriving isn't about having a perfect life. It's not about having zero problems, zero struggles, or some fairy-tale ending where everything magically falls into place. Thriving is about owning your life instead of life owning you.

It's when you wake up and realize you're not just surviving anymore; you're living.

262

Here's What Thriving Looks Like:

When you stop reacting to life and start creating it. You're no longer just putting out fires, waiting for the next disaster. You're making intentional choices instead of just doing what you're "supposed" to do.

When you stop needing permission to be happy, you don't wait for validation. You don't shrink yourself to make other people comfortable. Don't let guilt or fear take you out of the joy you deserve.

When you wake up, you no longer have to fight hard. Life still throws punches, but you're strong enough to handle them. You trust yourself in ways you never did before. You're no longer waiting for "one day," you're living right now.

How I Know Thriving Is Possible

My nonprofit and mental health careers have shown me things I didn't believe possible. I'm serious. If you only knew the thousands of horrendous stories my team and I have heard. The war people are waging behind their eyes. The fact is that mental distress can cause physical pain and vice versa. I have seen people walk away from their burning lives with smiles, their chests stuck out, and their heads high. Not because that giant explosion behind them just magically vanished, but because they know they survived. They know it happened. They know it changed them. They know they're different. Most importantly. They know they're still living. And the rest of their lives? They don't owe their past a single damn thing.

I've seen people who thought they'd never heal finally find

peace. I've seen people who swore they were failures, and they finally started thriving. I've seen people who thought they were broken beyond repair finally rebuild. And I've lived through enough of my shit, my trauma, and my own mistakes to know that it's possible for anyone.

Yes, even you. Thriving isn't about luck; it isn't about getting some perfect opportunity or waiting for the stars to align. It's about choosing, every single day, to show up for yourself. To fight for yourself. To believe you deserve more. To live fully, unapologetically, and on your terms. And the second you do that? That's when you thrive.

23

CHAPTER 23: APPLYING S.H.I.F.T. TO YOUR LIFE

This is why the S.H.I.F.T. Framework™ Exists

Every piece of this framework came from real life. Not from textbooks. Not from self-help trends. Not from some motivational guru selling "one-size-fits-all" solutions.

This came from the trenches. It came from watching people stay stuck and watching people break free. It came from working jobs that taught me what regret looks like. It came from watching people fight for themselves or give up entirely.

I've seen both sides of the coin. I've seen people who had every opportunity to change but never did because they were too afraid, conditioned, or exhausted to believe in something better. And I've seen people who had every excuse to stay down, every reason to quit, but chose to fight anyway. And that's the difference. Not intelligence. Not talent. Not luck.

What is the difference between those who change their lives and those who don't?

It's the decision to S.H.I.F.T.

The Hardest Part: Realizing You Are the Only One Who Can Save Yourself

Let's be honest; there is no easy way out. No magic shortcut. No secret key. No hero is coming to pull you out of your hell. Do you think therapists "fix" people? No. And if you've been told that, you've been lied to. Therapists help you uncover the parts of yourself that already exist. They don't solve your problems, they help you develop and refine the necessary skills to do so yourself. I am not fully licensed yet; however, I help people in this capacity daily as a resident.

I don't **fix** people. I **reveal** them.

Most people stay stuck because they're waiting to be rescued. They're waiting for the right moment. They're waiting for permission. They're waiting for life to suddenly become more manageable, for the universe to deliver them a perfect, struggle-free path.

That's not how this shit burger works. If you're waiting for someone to permit you to start living your own life, it's not coming. If you keep waiting? If you keep putting it off? If you keep telling yourself, "I'll change later, when I have more time, when I'm less tired, when I feel ready..."

Then, you're choosing to stay precisely where you are.

And you might not realize it yet, but that's a choice.

266

The Cost of Staying the Same vs. The Cost of Changing

There are two prices in life.

The price of staying the same.

Waking up every day feeling stuck. Knowing you're capable of more but doing nothing about it. Letting fear run your life and call the shots. Carrying regret so heavy, you feel it in your bones.

The price of changing.

The discomfort of breaking habits. The pain of unlearning old beliefs. The fear of stepping into the unknown. The challenge of becoming someone new. One of these will hurt.

One will cost you something, while the other will lead you somewhere worth going.

Which price are you willing to pay?

S.H.I.F.T. Exists Because You Deserve More

This framework isn't just words on a page. It's not some "feel-good" concept to nod to before returning to your regularly scheduled programming. It's a blueprint. For breaking cycles. For reclaiming your power. For refusing to be another person who dies full of regret. Every single step of S.H.I.F.T. exists because I have lived it.

Because I have sat in rooms with people who thought they were beyond saving and watched them prove themselves wrong. I have been the person who felt like nothing would ever change until I stopped waiting for something outside of me to fix it. I have met people at rock bottom who were seconds away from giving up, who made one decision, one shift, that changed everything.

And now? It's in front of you. You can ignore it. You can close this book. You can keep doing what you've always done. And in five years, when nothing has changed, you can tell yourself, "I guess that's just life."

Or. You can decide right now that this is your turning point. That you are done waiting. That you are done making excuses. You are done living small, settling for less, and convincing yourself that "maybe this is just how things are." Because it's not.

But no one can make that decision for you. No one is coming to save you. You can save yourself.

How to Apply S.H.I.F.T. to Any Area of Life

The beauty of S.H.I.F.T. is that it works everywhere.

This isn't some abstract theory meant for motivational speeches and Instagram captions. This is a battle plan, a framework you can apply to any aspect of your life that feels stuck, broken or needs a serious overhaul. Whether it's your mindset, your career, your relationships, your habits, your self-worth, or your entire damn life, S.H.I.F.T. works.

But here's the catch: You have to apply it.

Applying S.H.I.F.T. to Your Mindset

Your mind is your biggest weapon or your biggest enemy.

If your thoughts are working against you, nothing else you do will matter. So, before anything else, you've got to S.H.I.F.T. your mindset.

S: STOP

Stop feeding self-doubt every time you second-guess yourself. Stop talking to yourself like you're a failure. Stop allowing toxic beliefs (from society, family, and past experiences) to dictate your worth.

H: HYPE

Hype yourself up like you would your best friend. No more self-deprecation disguised as "humor." Affirm your value— even if it feels awkward at first. "I am capable. I am worth it. I am the main character."

I: INNOVATE

Reinvent the way you talk to yourself. Would you say that shit to someone you love? No? Then why the hell do you say it to yourself? Change how you handle failure; stop seeing it as the end and start seeing it as data. If something doesn't work, adjust, don't quit. Control what you can, and adapt to the rest.

F: FIGHT

Fight against negative self-talk. Catch yourself in the act and reframe the thought. Fight against comparison. You're running your race. Stay in your damn lane.

T: THRIVE

Make peace with who you are while still growing into the person you want to become. Permit yourself to feel joy, confidence, and success without guilt.

Applying S.H.I.F.T. to Your Career & Goals

Feeling stuck in your job? Lost in your purpose? Let's S.H.I.F.T. that shit.

S: STOP

Stop settling for a job that's draining your soul just because it's "secure." Stop waiting for the "perfect time" to go after what you want. It doesn't exist. Stop giving fear more power than your dreams.

H: HYPE

Remind yourself why you started. Even if the path has changed, your worth and ambition haven't. Speak about your work, skills, and aspirations with confidence. No more "Oh, I just do [insert downplaying]." Own your greatness.

I: INNOVATE

Change how you approach success. If the traditional path isn't working, create your own. Adapt, learn, evolve, try new skills, network differently, take a leap. Comfort zones don't build legacies.

F: FIGHT

Fight for what you deserve-better pay, a new role, or a career pivot. Fight through imposter syndrome. Nobody has it all figured out. What is the difference between success and stagnation? People who do it anyway.

T: THRIVE

Find a way to make your work fulfilling through impact, creativity, or freedom. Define what success looks like to YOU, not what society says it should be.

Applying S.H.I.F.T. to Relationships (Romantic, Friendships, Family, etc.)

The relationships in your life should energize you, not drain you. Time to S.H.I.F.T. the way you approach connections.

S: STOP

Stop tolerating half-assed effort, manipulative people, or emotional parasites. Stop expecting people to change when they've made it clear they won't.

H: HYPE

Hype up your damn standards. You deserve respect, effort, and reciprocity. Speak life into your relationships. Be a person who encourages, uplifts, and inspires.

I: INNOVATE

Change how you approach relationships. If you're constantly in toxic cycles, look at your patterns, your boundaries, and your choices. Try new ways to connect, have deeper conversations, engage in active listening, and show up differently.

F: FIGHT

Fight for relationships worth keeping. The best connections aren't effortless; they're built. Fight against old wounds dictating new relationships.

T: THRIVE

Surround yourself with people who challenge, support, and love you fully. Be in relationships (romantic or platonic) that allow you to grow and evolve together.

Applying S.H.I.F.T. to Health & Well-Being

Your body and mind? Non-negotiable. Time to S.H.I.F.T. the way you treat them.

S: STOP

Stop treating self-care as a luxury. It's a necessity. Stop the cycle of neglect, burnout, and exhaustion.

H: HYPE

Hype yourself up no matter where you are on your journey. Progress is progress. Speak kindly about your body. It hears you.

I: INNOVATE

Find new ways to move, eat, and care for yourself that feel good. Ditch the all-or-nothing mindset. Progress beats perfection.

F: FIGHT

Fight for your well-being. Nobody else will do it for you. Fight against guilt for putting yourself first.

T: THRIVE

Make your well-being a lifestyle, not a phase. Learn to love taking care of yourself.

Applying S.H.I.F.T. to Self-Worth & Identity

Who are you? Let's make sure you like the answer.

S: STOP

Stop basing your worth on external validation, achievements, or approval. Stop apologizing for who you are.

H: HYPE

Hype yourself up as your life depends on it because it does. Affirm your value daily.

I: INNOVATE

Change how you see yourself. You're not just your past, your mistakes, or your insecurities. Try new experiences that expand your understanding of yourself.

F: FIGHT

Fight against old programming that says you're "not enough." Fight for the version of you that refuses to shrink.

T: THRIVE

Live fully, loudly, unapologetically. Own your story, your truth, and your power.

For My First Responders

I hope you've made it this far. Like many of you, I spent years behind the wheel of a patrol car, answering calls that tore lives apart, watching people break in front of me, and carrying things home that I wouldn't wish on anyone. I know what it's like to wear the uniform, to carry the weight of everyone else's emergencies while pretending you're fine. And now, in my work with peer support, mental health, and trauma recovery, I've sat across from first responders who are barely holding it together. Remarkable people who've spent their careers saving others, but don't know how to save themselves. That's why I built the S.H.I.F.T. Framework™. Not because it looks good on paper, but because it works in real life. It's for those of us who have seen the worst in humanity, who've answered the calls nobody else can handle, and who are ready to stop surviving and start living again. I mean seriously, consider the hundreds of people who still walk this planet or who get to enjoy the rest of their time here because you intervened in their life. YOU! If you don't think you deserve to heal, to live life to the absolute fullest, the world has failed you. You didn't fail it. Because despite your demons, you still serve. Despite your pain, you still show up. Despite everything that continues to push against you, you push back. You hold in your heart the very character that Hollywood aims to portray in superheroes. But you're rarely treated that way. Start saving yourself the way you save others. Somewhere along the way, you may have forgotten that you deserve everything you give to everyone else. S.H.I.F.T.

The Job Can Save Lives. Don't Let It Take Yours.

S: STOP

Stop sacrificing yourself for the job.

Stop ignoring the warning signs, burnout, fatigue, anger, numbness.

Stop telling yourself you're fine when you're not.

H: HYPE

Back yourself the way you back your crew.

Remind yourself: you've survived 100% of your worst days.

You are not weak for needing support, you're smart for asking for it.

I: INNOVATE

Change how you cope.

The old ways, stuff it down, drink it away, aren't working.

Try something different. Peer support. Counseling. Moving your body.

Reinvent your recovery. It's okay for the helper to need help.

F: FIGHT

Fight for yourself the way you fight for everyone else.

Fight for your life after the badge, the engine, the squad, and the headset.

Fight for your family, for your future, for your peace.

T: THRIVE

Thrive beyond the uniform.

You are not your job. You are not your job. You are not your job.

Did I say you are not your job?

You can have peace, purpose, and freedom, on your terms.

But What If I Don't Know Where I'm Going?

I get it. Maybe you don't have the whole plan laid out yet. Do any of us? Perhaps you're thinking, "What if I make the wrong turn?" Would you rather be somewhat lost and moving or completely stuck and miserable? Because the truth is, there is no perfect route. Even people who seem like they "have it all figured out" are just guessing with confidence. Do you think because I wrote this book that, I have all my shit together? Please. My brain is a never-ending construction zone, with cones everywhere, detours popping up from nowhere, and the occasional traffic jam of overthinking. But guess what? I keep driving. Because motion, even fraught, chaotic, holy-shit-where-am-I motion, is better than sitting in the same damn spot waiting for a sign that isn't coming.

Life isn't about perfect navigation. It's about course correction. Did you take a wrong turn? So what? Adjust. Recalculate. Keep moving. Stagnation is absolute failure, not making mistakes. You don't need the whole map. You need the guts to put the car in drive and figure it out as you go. You don't need a damn five-year plan. You don't need to wait for "more clarity." You don't need a sign from the universe. You need to start moving.

Because movement creates momentum. And momentum? That's what gets you unstuck.

Have you ever tried steering a parked car? You can spin the wheel all you want, but you're not going anywhere until you hit the gas. So don't wait for the universe to slide a GPS under your door.

Pick a direction. Start moving. Adjust as needed.

It's Time to S.H.I.F.T.

"I'll start when I'm ready." → No, you won't. Readiness is a myth. "I just need a little more time." → Time doesn't change you. Action does. "But what if I fail?" → What if you don't? What if this works? Waiting is a trap.

And if you've been waiting for some magical moment where everything clicks, you suddenly feel 100% ready? That moment doesn't exist.

So, stop stalling. Stop hesitating. Stop looking for reasons to stay parked.

Not because you have everything figured out. Not because the road ahead is obvious. Not because you feel ready. But because you refuse to stay stuck. Because you are done waiting. Changing your life is realizing that trying to drive while using the lens of a rearview mirror will cause you to crash way before it gets you to your destination.

24

CHAPTER 24: YOU'RE THE S.H.I.F.T. SHOW

You always have been.

Because this isn't just a book, you're not just a reader. It's all the secrets and discomfort you've ignored. All the pain you've chosen to carry. All the hate that poisons you. All the things that we SHOULD be focused on and all the bullshit that's unworthy of our attention. It's a wake-up call. And you? You're the one holding the alarm clock. You're not just a passenger in this life; you're the damn driver. Every excuse, every hesitation, every maybe later is just you handing over the keys to someone else. But guess what? No one's coming to steer for you. No one will permit you to live the life you want.

This is it. You're the S.H.I.F.T. Show. The chaos, the breakthroughs, the stumbles, the wins, it's all you. So, what are you going to do with it? Keep watching from the sidelines, or finally step into the main event? It's about learning that you have the power to not only carry yourself through the gauntlet of this unexplainable cluster fuck of life, but that you have the power to save it. One person, one conversation, one altered perspective, and one changed opinion at a time.

Your voice can make all the difference. Your actions can stop the fighting—the fighting in your head and the fighting among us.

Speaking Of Fighting

Millions of people don't have clean drinking water. Why are we fighting? Cancer, heart disease, violence, abuse, and mental illness destroy families every day. Why are we fighting? Billionaires eat thousand-dollar meals while children eat from dumpsters. Why are we fighting? It's 2025, and people are sold into slavery. Sex slavery. Children. Why are we fighting? Some people will never hear the words "I love you." Why are we fighting? War wipes entire cities off the map. Why are we fighting? Natural disasters kill hundreds of thousands at a time. Why are we fighting? Children are murdered in our schools. Why are we fighting? There are tragedies every .001 seconds. Why are we fighting? Our world is on fire, drowning, shaking, and breaking. Why are we fighting?

We are all the same. We all hurt, bleed, cry, win, lose, succeed, fail, do right, and do wrong. We all have embarrassing traits we try to hide. We all have stories we want to tell. We all want to be loved. We all want to be happy. We are all wonderfully, weirdly, and beautifully made. Sometimes we're great, sometimes we suck. Be we are always...We. Why the fuck are we fighting?

We all find ourselves on this spinning rock of dirt, water, and shit, trying to figure out who we are, why we're here, what the hell we're doing, what the hell happens next, and everything in between. None of us have it all figured out. None of us are without problems. None of us have it all together. None of us deserve to suffer. None of us deserve hate. None of us deserve the terrible things that have happened to us.

We all deserve love. We all deserve peace. We all deserve happiness. We all deserve freedom. We all deserve the same rights. We all deserve safety. We all deserve to heal. We all deserve to grow. We all deserve to S.H.I.F.T.

It doesn't matter if your skin is dark, your God is white, your love is gay, or your house is big. Whether your car is brand new or held together with duct tape and prayers. It doesn't matter if your bank account is stacked or hanging on by a decimal point. It doesn't matter if you drink oat milk or straight-up whole milk. It doesn't matter if you wear designer labels or if your favorite hoodie is held together by sheer willpower and nostalgia.

Your piss still hits the water just like everyone else's. You still pick your nose when no one's looking, scroll through things you'd rather not admit, and miscalculate the width of a doorway at least once in your life.

You've sent a text, then immediately put your phone on silent and thrown it across the room like a grenade. You've sat on the toilet far longer than necessary to get a break from people. You've rehearsed arguments in the shower, an entire monologue, and an Oscar-worthy performance, only to get into real-life conflict and say, "Okay."

You've liked a post, then unliked it because you realized it was from 2017, and now you look like a stalker. You've waved back at someone who wasn't waving at you and committed to it fully. You've nodded in conversations where you had no idea what was happening.

You've refreshed an app like it owed you money. You've

Googled something weird and immediately cleared your history like the FBI was on standby. You've laid in bed at night and remembered something embarrassing from middle school so vividly it made your stomach hurt.

You've let out a cough in a quiet room and accidentally turned it into a dramatic choking episode. You've confidently walked into a room, then immediately turned around because you forgot why you were there.

You've accidentally replied out loud to someone who was talking on their Bluetooth. You've tried to pull open a door that says "PUSH" in big, capital letters and then do it again to make sure it meant it.

You've put your card in the chip reader, tapped it, swiped it, then pretended to understand what the cashier meant when they said, "Try again." You've dropped your phone on your face while texting in bed. You've stared at a sock on the floor for days, fully capable of picking it up, yet somehow just... didn't.

But we all pretend we don't.

Strip away the labels, the facades, and the performative bullshit, and what are we? We are just a bunch of clumsy, insecure, beautifully flawed humans trying to make sense of this mess.

Now, you have a choice. You can close this, nod, and return to life as usual. You can keep running the same patterns, having the same arguments, holding the same grudges, and believing the same lies about yourself, others, and the world.

Or. You Can S.H.I.F.T.

You can take everything you've unpacked, the grief, the rage, the exhaustion, the self-doubt, the fear, the hate that was never really yours to carry, and you can choose differently. Because it is a choice.

Hate is a choice. Love is a choice. Bitterness is a choice. Compassion is a choice.

And I need you to hear me when I say this: You were not put on this earth to be at war with yourself. You were not put on this earth to be at war with other people. I don't care where you come from, what you believe, what you've done, what's been done to you. I don't care how many mistakes you've made or how many people have let you down. I don't care what labels you wear or which side of the imaginary lines this world has drawn to keep us divided you happen to stand on.

You are human. Worthy of love.

So is everyone else.

Everyone you've been taught to fear, hate, judge, dismiss. Every person whose life, struggles, or identity you've never fully understood. Every person who has made mistakes. Every person who is doing their best to survive. And yeah, I get it; some people make it hard to believe. Some people are awful. Some people hurt others. Some people carry so much hate inside them that it spills onto everyone they touch.

But if we fight hate with more hate? If we match judgment with more judgment? If we let our wounds turn us into the very thing we despise? Then we lose.

Not just as individuals. Not just as a generation. As a species. Remember one of the biggest scams in history? The greatest lie ever sold to humanity?

We are meant to be divided and spend our lives tearing each other apart instead of lifting each other up. Kindness is a weakness. Compassion is naïve. Power comes from control instead of connection. That we are not all in this together.

But we are. We always have been, and we are running out of time to start acting like it. Everywhere you look, people are hurting. People are lonely. People are struggling under the weight of things they never asked for, never deserved, never should have had to carry alone. And you, right now, you have the power to change that.

Not by fixing the whole world overnight. Not by winning some giant, flashy war against hate and cruelty. But by changing one moment. By choosing different, small, everyday ways that include seeing people, really seeing them. By offering kindness when you can provide indifference, by choosing understanding over judgment, and by speaking life into people who are drowning in doubt, By being the person who says, I don't have to agree with you to respect you. I don't have to understand you to treat you with kindness. I don't have to know your whole story to give a damn about how it ends.

Because that? That is what will change the world. Not politicians. Not institutions. Not another war, another law, another empty promise from people in power who will never give a shit about us.

Us. We are the shift. We always have been.

So, here's a challenge for you. When you wake up tomorrow, choose love. When you don't know what to say, choose kindness. When you're face-to-face with someone you don't understand, someone you disagree with, someone who has been painted as your enemy, choose humanity. And when you look in the mirror and hear the voice in your head trying to convince you that you're not enough, that you're unworthy, that you'll never be whole, choose yourself.

Because the moment we all start doing that?

The world shifts.

Everything changes.

And it starts with you.

So, I encourage you to:

Drink your coffee. Mind your business. Be curious, not judgmental. Ask people how they're doing and listen to the answer. Laugh more. Harder. Cry when you need to. No, seriously. Cry. Your body is trying to get rid of stress hormones. Let it.

Stop making yourself small for people who wouldn't shrink for you. Unlearn the bullshit society has drilled into you. Rest when you're tired. Take up space. Take the damn compliment. Take the damn chance.

Dance like no one's watching. And if they are, make eye contact and make it weird. Don't give it your energy if it doesn't bring you peace, joy, or money. Say "no" without over-explaining yourself. Say "yes" to what scares the hell out of you.

Stop waiting for life to happen to you, and start happening to your life! Hug the people you love. Tell them you love them. Life is too short for ego. Let people be who they are. If they're not hurting anyone, let them live their damn life.

Forgive, not because they deserve it, but because you deserve peace. Cut off people who drain you. You are not required to set yourself on fire to keep others warm. Don't let your past define your future. At any moment, you can decide to be someone new.

Remember that nobody knows what they're doing, so stop thinking you're the only one lost. We are all the same, chaotic, Topsy-turvy, figuring-it-out humans trying to navigate a world that makes no sense half the time.

Be kind. Be real. Be loud. Be soft. Be you.

There are so many things in life working against us. Let's stop causing additional turbulence on an already bumpy flight. The world sucks. Let's love ourselves and others despite it.

You are not your name, not your past, not your beliefs. Every single thing you think makes you "you" was given to you by someone else. Strip it all away, and what's left? Not some enlightened, poetic bullshit. Just you. Raw, accurate, and enough. This world has spent your entire existence trying to erase someone who knows who they are. Such a person that no system, fear, or lie can control.

You've seen the Shit Show. Are you going to continue contributing to it?

Or will you be the S.H.I.F.T. Show in a world gone to shit?

The Legacy of One

One person. That's all it takes. Not a movement. Not a revolution. Not a headline. Just one person deciding, really deciding, to care. To see someone who has been overlooked, dismissed, or forgotten. To step in when it would be easier to look away. To give a damn in a world that constantly tells you not to.

One person reaches out, and because of that, someone barely holding on doesn't let go. Someone who thought their story was over finds the strength to turn the page. Someone who believed they were invisible suddenly realizes that they exist, that they matter, and that their life is not just something happening—it's something worth exploring.

And that person, the one who was saved? They don't just carry on. They carry forward.

Because impact is like wildfire, it spreads.

The Chain Reaction of One Small Choice

Maybe that person saves two others—not by some grand gesture or heroic act, but by doing what was done for them, by showing up. They sit with someone who is drowning in silence. They remind them they are not alone through words, presence, or simply refusing to leave.

Now, those two? They carry six. And those six carry thirty. And those thirty? They step out into a world conditioned to break people down and do something radical: They build.

Maybe one of them is a teacher who tells a kid, "You are capable. You are enough. You are more than what life has convinced you you're destined for."

Maybe one is a stranger who notices someone on the edge of their breaking point and says,

"Hey. You good?"

Maybe one is a parent who breaks the cycle, teaches love instead of fear, and raises a child who will never have to recover from the damage they had to survive.

Now, imagine what happens when this doesn't stop. Imagine someone, two hundred years after you're gone, living a life that would not have existed if not for you. Not because you

287

were famous. Not because you were powerful. Not because you were rich, brilliant, or had all the answers.

But because, in one moment, you chose to care. You decided to give a shit for someone who felt like shit. Who believed bullshit. Who shit on themselves. Who shit on others.

Giving a shit is cool. Normalize giving a shit. More shits, please.

The Truth You'll Never Fully See

You will never see the full weight of what you did in this world. You will never know every life touched because you decided to be a force for something better.

But make no mistake, the effect of what you do in this world will outlive you. The kind word that stopped a downward spiral. The hand that reached out before someone let go—the moment you made someone feel seen when they felt invisible.

Maybe you'll never hear about it. Perhaps you'll never get credit for it. Maybe you'll never know the difference you made. But the difference was made.

Because legacies are not built in monuments but built in moments.

You Get to Choose What You Leave Behind

Life is fleeting. Everything we build, everything we accumulate, everything we hoard, it all fades. But impact? That shit stays long after your voice goes quiet. Long after, your name is forgotten. Long after history moves on without you, your presence will still echo. Your choices will still ripple. Your kindness will still move through people you never even met.

Because long after you are gone, the waves you created will still move.

You won't see the final wave.

But you will have been the first drop.

So, Here's Your Final Challenge:

Make it count. Make your words count. Make your love count. Make your time count. Make your pain count. Make your laughter count. Make your choices count. Make your failures count. Make your lessons count. Make your kindness count. Make your presence count. Make your resilience count. Make your existence count. Make your risks count. Make your growth count. Make your scars count. Make your voice count. Make your joy count. Make your truth count. Make your second chances count. Make your defiance count. Make your legacy count.

Because this all ends.

And in the time you're here? You get to decide what you leave behind.

Your voice. Your choice.

One day, you will take your last breath. And in that moment, nothing will matter, no opinions, failures, or fears, except whether you genuinely lived. So, stop waiting. Love recklessly, speak your truth, chase what sets your soul on fire, and leave no part of yourself unexplored. The only thing worse than dying is reaching the end and realizing you never truly lived. You are the only person who will be with you from your first breath to your last, so make sure you are someone you can be proud of.

Spending a little time with you on your journey has been one of my life's great privileges. Out of billions of years, infinite possibilities, and countless stars that burned and died before you were ever a thought, here you are. The odds of you existing precisely as you are now are so impossibly small that you are, by every definition, a miracle. So don't waste a second of this rare, unrepeatable life, dimming yourself to fit a world never meant to contain you.

If you blew through these pages or if the weight of their content is all just a blur at this point, please hear this. Sit with it. Digest it. Process it.

A day will come when your body will fail you.

A day will come when your mind will fail you.

A day will come when your loved ones will be gone.

A day will come when your next......won't.

You may have 100 years left.

You may have 3 minutes.

Love who loves you.

Forget the rest.

You are not an idea.

When you stand before the mirror, recognize that your reflection is not just flesh and form—it is the manifestation of unseen forces, woven from the infinite and the inexplicable, shaping you into something only the universe could conceive.

Your life means something. Something to someone. Something to you.

You are an unrepeatable phenomenon—a singular fusion of experiences, resilience, and untold potential, woven into existence with a purpose only you can fulfill.

Don't waste you. There will never be another. Your mark deserves to be left—because someone, somewhere, is waiting for the shift that only you can create.

Enjoy your S.H.I.F.T. Show. Enjoy loving yourself in a world that won't. It's a hell of a feeling.

About the Author

My name is Adam. I am an observer of the human struggle, and I've experienced it from multiple angles.

I've been on the front lines of chaos and crisis. As a state trooper, I saw what happens when people break. When life, circumstance, and split-second decisions push them past the point of no return. I've witnessed the best and worst of humanity, stood in the middle of moments most people never have to see, and learned just how thin the line is between "having it together" and crashing into the rocks.

Now, in mental health, I help people pick up the pieces. I work with first responders, trauma survivors, and anyone who knows what it feels like to carry burdens too heavy to hold alone. I've spent years walking alongside people in pain that words can't explain—the silent battles, unbearable grief, and the unspoken fears that keep people stuck in the mud.

With a master's in clinical counseling, I am in residency and pursuing a PhD in Trauma-Informed Care. I also have credentials in Critical Incident Stress Management (CCISM) and have worked with hundreds of first responders from across the state, country, and world, helping them navigate the weight of their humanity in a world that expects them to be unbreakable, emotionless machines.

My experience with struggle isn't just professional; it's personal.

I know what it's like to question everything. Including life itself. To wonder if change is possible. To feel trapped by the past, circumstances, and a world that thrives on keeping people stuck. I've been there. I've fought through it. I still am, and I try to help others do the same.

That's why I created the S.H.I.F.T. Framework ™. Not just as another self-help formula but as a wake-up call. A blueprint for breaking cycles, seeing through the bullshit, and taking back the power that was never meant to be handed over in the first place.

When I'm not traveling around the state looking for the next soul to hopefully leave a positive impact on, you'll catch me throwing a little boy in the air, laughing with the funniest person I know, snuggling with an army of dogs, and trying to figure out what the hell we're all doing.

You can connect with me on:
- https://x.com/SHIFTshowbook
- https://www.facebook.com/adamblevinsauthor
- https://www.facebook.com/welcometotheshiftshow
- https://www.instagram.com/officialwelcometotheshiftshow